SKIATHOS

SKOPELOS &
ALONNISOS

EDITIONS
TOUBI'S
ΕΚΔΟΣΕΙΣ

Text on Skiathos: BETTY KAGIA
Text on Skopelos and Alonisos: YIANNIS DESYPRIS
Natural environment: YIORGOS SFIKAS
Geological details: VASILIS TSELEPIDIS
Text editing: DAPHNE CHRISTOU
Photography: MICHALIS TOUBIS S.A. FILES
Artistic supervision: EVI DAMIRI
Translation: JUDY GIANNAKOPOULOU

Copyright © 2000 MICHALIS TOUBIS S.A.
519 Vouliagmenis Ave, Ilioupoli 163 41, Tel: (01) 9923876, Fax 9923867, Athens
Internet: http://www.toubis.gr
ISBN: 960-540-385-4

We would like to express our warmest thanks for their advice during the writing of this book to: the Development Organisation of Skiathos, the Skopelos Folk Museum, the Society for the Study and Protection of the Mediterranean Seal, Mrs Athina Papageorgiou member of the artistic committee for the events "Dream on the Wave".

*"Because of course the land of innocence
is not as some people would imagine;
it has its saints and savages,
its virgin forests and calm waters."*

ODYSSEUS ELYTIS
(The Magic of Papadiamantis)

CONTENTS

1. SKIATHOS

2. HISTORY

3. CULTURE & TRADITION

4. TOUR OF HORA & THE KASTRO

CONTENTS

Skiathos, the most cosmopolitan and best known of the Northern Sporades, is an island that has been endowed by nature as have few others; it has also been blessed by the people who live on it. Its position, remote from the bustling tourism of the central Aegean, has protected the island's unique character. The vegetation that covers almost the entire island with pine forests, such as the one at Aradias, and countless olive groves, vineyards and other crops, gives it a unique colour, as the dense greenery extends as far as the shore where it touches the crystal waters of the beaches round the island, each one different. Here the power of the sea and time have created works of unique beauty, especially on the virgin northern coasts of the island, carving out caves, and sculpting rocks and coves that are a source of delight to its many visitors, whether they are from other parts of Greece or from abroad. At every moment of the day, the touch of the Greek sun on the clear waters of the Aegean Sea creates an ever-changing kaleidescope of colour and light. The southern coasts of Skiathos, which are much more hospitable and accessible, conceal yet another picture of the Aegean's multiple natural diversity. The island's two ponds, at Hora and Koukounaries, are also welcoming, as they constitute important wetland habitats in the Greek ecosystem with a great variety of indigenous birds as well as migratory species that voyage every year from north to south and back. In such a cordial and fertile land, it would be impossible for man, too, not to thrive, both in his ordinary everyday life and in his intellectual life as well.

The stability that Skiathos gives to its inhabitants and to their culture, despite the terrible hardships they have occasionally had to face from ancient times until the present, can be seen clearly in the fact that the island still retains its first, ancient name: Skiathos. The diamond of the Northern Sporades.

Skiathos:
full of surprises and promises.

Koukounaries.

Geography

Skiathos is situated right in the middle of the northwestern Aegean, the westernmost island of the Northern Sporades archipelago. On the west it is bordered by the coasts of Magnesia, from which it is separated by the Skiathos Channel (minimum width 3.8 km) and to the east by the island of Skopelos, with the Skopelos Channel dividing them. The main ports serving Skiathos' shipping communication with mainland Greece are Ayios Konstantinos, which is 44 miles away, and Volos, 41 miles away.

Near Skiathos there is a multitude of islands large and small: Skopelos, Alonnisos, Skyros to the south, and all around are Peristera, Kyra-Panayia, Yioura, Skantzoura, Piperi, Psathoura, Tsougria and its Tsougraki, Aspronisi, Maragos, Arkos, the Kastronisia, the Troulonisia and the Myrmigonisia.

The island is 61 sq km in area, with a perimeter of 48 km. The greater part of it (70% of the terrain) is mountainous. The highest mountain on Skiathos is Karafiltzanaka in the north, its peak Stavros at an altitude of 433 m.

Skiathos is irregular in shape (12 km long and 6 km wide from north to south), with coasts offering an interesting horizon as well as vertical stratification. Some 70 bays and inlets are created as well as many peninsulas. In the rugged and inaccessible northwestern part is cape Kastro. To the west, the bay of Katavothras is formed by the capes of Sozon and Gournes. In the southwest is cape Pounta, east of which are the bays of Koukounaries and Platanias with their wonderful golden sands. Farther along, the little peninsula of Kanapitsa terminates in cape Kalamaki. To the southeast of the island is the town of Skiathos, on the western shore of the bay of the same name. The landscape is serene in the southern part of the island, in contrast with its craggy northern and eastern parts. In the northern section, there are caves with names like Skoteini (Dark), Galazia (Azure) and Halkini (Bronze), as well as Trypia Petra (Rock with a Hole).

The island boasts an excellent climate, with mild winters and quite a high rainfall. During the summer months, there is a lot of sunlight and warm weather from April to October, although the summer winds (meltemia) that blow in the northern Aegean help to reduce the high temperatures.

In recent years, the economy of Skiathos has been based mainly on the tourist trade and fishing, to the neglect of crop and livestock farming. Indeed, the island is considered to be among the most highly developed of the Northern Sporades from the point of view of tourist facilities, and can provide good services through its satisfactory infrastructure and organisation.

Ecclesiastically Skiathos belongs to the Metropolis of Halkida (formerly known as Chalcis). It has 5096 inhabitants (1991 census) most of whom live in Hora, the island's capital and main port, with fewer living in the countryside.

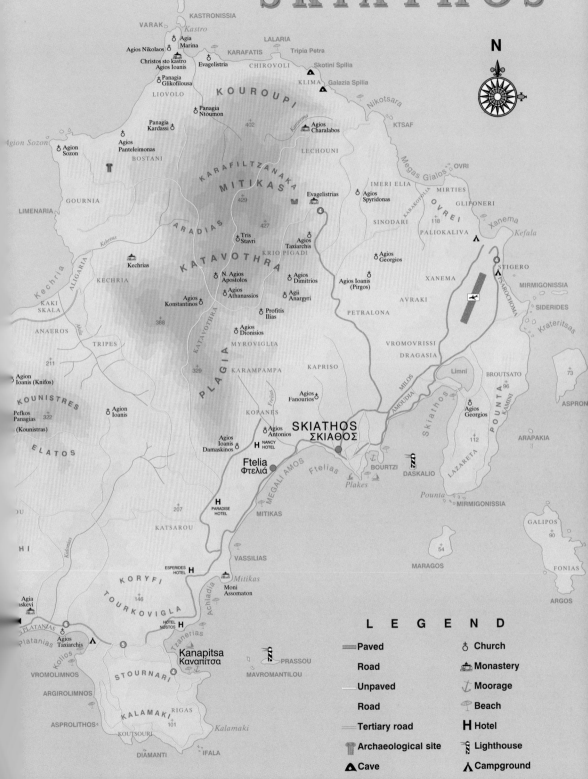

SKIATHOS

N

KASTRONISSIA
VARAK
Kastro
Agios Nikolaos — Agia Marina
Christos sto kastro
Agios Ioanis
Evagelistria
LALARIA
Tripia Petra
KARAFATIS
CHIROVOLI
Skotini Spilia
Panagia Glikofilousa
KLIMA
Galazia Spilia
LIOVOLO
KOUROUPI
Nikotsara
Panagia Ntoumon
KTSAF
Panagia Kardassi
402
Karampa
Agios Charalabos
Agios Panteleimonas
LECHOUNI
Agion Sozon
Agion Sozon
BOSTANI
KARAFILTZANAKA
MITIKAS
Megas Gialos
OVRI
MIRTIES
GLIFONERI
IMERI ELIA
Evagelistrias
Agios Spyridonas
OVREI
LIMENARIA
GOURNIA
429
SINODARI
118
Xanema
Kefala
ARADIAS
427
PALIOKALIVA
Tris Stavri
Agios Taxiarchis
KRIO PIGADI
STIGERO
KATAVOTHRA
Kechrias
N. Agios Apostolos
Agios Athanassios
Agios Dimitriou
Agios Georgios
Agios Ioanis (Pirgos)
Xanema
MIRMIGONISSIA
SIDERIDES
KECHRIA
Agios Konstantinos
Agii Anargyri
AVRAKI
Kratritsas
KAKI SKALA
388
Profitis Ilias
PETRALONA
ANAEROS
Agios Dionisios
MYROVIGLIA
211
TRIPES
329
KARAMPAMBA
VROMOVRISSI
DRAGASIA
73
ASPRON
Agion Ioanis (Knifos)
PLAGIA
KAPRISO
Limni
BROUTSATO
96
Pefkos Panagias
322
Agion Ioanis
KOPANES
Agios Fanourios
MILOS
Agios Georgios
ARAPAKIA
(Kounistras)
ELATOS
Agios Antonios
SKIATHOS
ΣΚΙΑΘΟΣ
112
AMOUDIA
Skiathos
LAZARETA
POUNTA
KAMINI
Agios Ioanis Damaskinos
NANCY HOTEL
BOURTZI
DASKALIO
GALIPOS
90
Ftelia
Φτελιά
MEGALI AMOS
Ftelias
Plakes
Pounta
MIRMIGONISSIA
PARADISE HOTEL
207
MITIKAS
54
MARAGOS
FONIAS
KATSAROU
VASSILIAS
ESPERIDES HOTEL
KORYFI
146
Mitikas
Moni Assomaton
Agia askevi
TOURKOVIGLA
Achladia
HOTEL NOSTOS
Platanias
6
Agios Taxiarchis
5
Tzanerias
Kanapitsa
Καναπίτσα
PRASSOU
MAVROMANTILOU
VROMOLIMNOS
STOURNARI
4
ARGIROLIMNOS
KALAMAKI
RIGAS
101
Kalamaki
ASPROLITHOS
KOUTSOURI
DIAMANTI
IFALA
ARGOS

L E G E N D

Paved Road	☦ Church
Unpaved Road	⛪ Monastery
Tertiary road	⚓ Moorage
Archaeological site	🏖 Beach
▲ Cave	**H** Hotel
	🗼 Lighthouse
	Λ Campground

Geology

Geologically, the island of Skiathos belongs to the pelagonic tectonic zone. The oldest rocks on the island belong to the Late Palaeozoic geological era. They include gneiss, amphibolite schist and amphibolites, i.e. metamorphic rocks that have been subjected to great pressure and high temperatures. The gneisses and gneiss-schists contain feldspar, mica and quartz and are found in the southwestern part of the island. These strata have gone through many stages of metamorphosis. The first stage took place in the Palaeozoic era, the second in the Mesozoic era around the Early Cretaceous geological epoch. On top of these strata is rock from the Triassic geological period consisting of schist of pyroclastic origin, mainly from quartz and epidote. Over these strata is marble from the middle Triassic to the Jurassic period, which is thickly stratified and even unstratified, from slate white to ash-coloured marble. In its lower sections, there are intrusions of dolomite marble and crystallic dolomites. Homogeneous marble can be seen only in the central and eastern parts of the island in isolated positions. The pelagonic zone closes with limestone that ranges from ash in colour to slate white, thin layers to unlayered, frequently bitumenous recrystallised and sometimes dolomitised rock of the Late Cretaceous period which are confined to the northeastern section of the island and appear only in isolated sites. They appear more frequently in the north-northeast part of the island, in the regions of Mytikas, Kambia and farther north at Kouroupi. Between the Late Jurassic and Early Cretaceous period, there was a thrust by rock strata on the markedly eroded pre-Cretaceous pelagonic series of formations. It consists of micaceous brown-grey limestone that contains deposits of phyllites, lenticles of post-volcanic and intercalations of recrystallised limestone. They occupy the entire northeastern section of the island. The town of Skiathos is built primarily on such formations. The island's more recent rock is argillaceous sandy material with smooth pebbles and shingles in the beds and estuaries of the ravines.

Flora - Fauna

The island of Skiathos is one of the most heavily forested islands in the Aegean, with pine, plane trees, oak and olive trees covering its entire area, as well as a great variety of shrubbery and wild plants. With respect to pine trees in particular, on Skiathos you'll find the species Pinus halepensis or Cyprus pine. Other flora include holly, myrtle, ferns, bulrushes and maquis, the classic Mediterranean scrub. Many years ago, all the pine forests on Skiathos were declared protected, and are among the nineteen "beautiful forests" in Greece. The forest of Skiathos extends mainly over the eastern part of the island and has an area of 3000 ha. Hunting, livestock grazing, and woodcutting are prohibited here, as are other activities that could alter its character.

To the southwest is the famous Koukounaries beach, a long sandy beach that terminates in a wonderful forest of Pinus pinea (koukounaria or stone pine). Behind this forest is a small wetland area. This region has been singled out as a landscape of particular natural beauty, and special measures have been taken by the Municipality of Skiathos to protect it. It should be noted that this stone pine forest is one of just three seaside Pinus pinea forests in Greece; in the entire Mediterranean there are no more than ten, which are regarded as rare habitats requiring protection.

The flora of Skiathos also includes many plant species that are common in Greece and in the Aegean, such as poppies, anemones, camomiles, etc. The only rare plant is the Campanula skiathia, a local variety of bellflower that grows on steep cliffs and even on stone walls right in the capital of the island.

The fauna of the island has not been studied in particular. During migration many birds stop over in the two ponds at Ayios Georgios and Strofylia at Koukounaries, including the Eleonora falcon, the Aegean gull, and the night heron. In addition, many birds of prey, terns and various species of herons use

Skiathos as a transit point in their migration, while ducks and even swans will spend the winter here. In the region around Mt Karafiltzanaka the many partridges of the Alectoris chukar *species remind us that in* antiquity the island was known for its choice partridges. Other birds encountered on the island are quail and turtle-dove and a few woodcocks in winter.

The flora on the island of Skiathos includes the rare species Campanula skiathia.

2

The island has always been called by the same name from the time of the geographer Strabo through that of the Emperor Constantine Porphyrogenitus (the Purple-born) and up to the modern age. The folk version of the origin of the name Skiathos is that it was derived from the shadow (skia) of Mt Athos, its land border to the north. Andreas Moustoxydis believed that the name was somehow related to Skia, a market town on Evia, from which the ancient Chalcidians set out to colonise Skiathos.

The Greek author Alexandros Papadiamantis, whose home was on the island, agreed with those who believed that the name Skiathos was pre-Hellenic and that it had been given to the island by its first settlers, the Pelasgians, who were impressed by the great shade (skia) provided by the trees. In fact, the Pelasgians were the first settlers of Skiathos, according to the Periigisin a work by an anonymous writer. They were a pre-Hellenic people who arrived on Skiathos from Thrace, moving southward during the great population movements of the Hellenic tribes. According to Thucydides, however, prior to all of them, the island was inhabited by the Carians, who had occupied many islands in the Aegean, from which Minos ejected them. After the Pelasgians, it was the Cretans and the Myceneans who occupied Skopelos (ancient Peparithos), Alonnisos (ancient Ikos), Skyros and others.

The god worshipped on this islands was Dionysus. One of his cult names was "Skianthos" which so resembles the island's name.

After the Cretans, who brought the cultivation of the olive and vine to Skiathos, settlers arrived from nearby Chalcis and found it deserted. During the Mycenean period the Thessalians came. Diodorus wrote that Pelias, before becoming king of Iolchus, conquered Skiathos and Skopelos and ruled on the islands for a period of time. Historical research reports that these first settlers lived on the site that is named today Erimo Horio (Deserted Village). Other

testimony reports that the pre-historic inhabitants built their cities on high ground, but near the sea. So it is thus possible that the ancient settlers of Skiathos may have built their town on the site where later the Chalcidians landed. A theory propounded by the historian A. Sampson holds

From the pre-historic period to modern times

that on the Kephala site on Skiathos there was a pre-historic settlement that flourished between 1000-700 BC. Sampson also stated that traces of buildings and ceramic shards were found there from the sub-Mycenean, Protogeometric and Geometric periods.

Skiathos. Copper plate print 12.7 x 16.7 cm. Gennadios Library, Athens.

Archaic period

Early in the 8th century BC, the inhabitants of Chalcis in Euboea (now called Halkida, Evia), Ionians in origin, began their colonising activities, as they had their eye on the island of Skiathos, off the north coast of their own island. When they began their expeditions northward in the direction of Chalcidice (now called Halkidiki) in the 7th or 6th c. BC, the opportunity presented itself. They captured Skiathos which they saw to be a fertile island and made it their colony, using its broad harbour as a base of operations. Later they planted trees, and developed the cultivation of olive and vine to such an extent and with such high quality produce that Skiathian wine became famous and began to be exported.

Almost all ancient geographers and historians agree that there was a town on the island. The geographer Strabo wrote that the island had a "city of the same name". Ptolemy said that it was an "island and town". Livy reported that there was just one flourishing town on the island but that it was destroyed by Philip of Macedonia. The historian Friedrich wrote that the shape of the island, its formation and the fertility of its soil argued in favour of there being just one town on Skiathos. The historian Philipson considered it doubtful whether there was a second town, and Tryphon Evangelides stated that indeed the island of Skiathos had only one town.

The Chalcidians, with their knowledge of the sea and of safe navigation, built the town of Skiathos southeast of the harbour, where there is a promontory that extends into the sea. The town looked out over the harbour and the sea. In front of the town was the bay and the inner harbour. But let us look at the town in terms of its present day sites and names. It started from Aï Yiannakis and continued indolently as far as the place called Limnia today. The town of Skiathos was surrounded by a strong protective wall. This wall, according to what the historians tell us, was built of square-cut blocks of marble. It had two gates and communicated with both the harbour and with the hinterland. This town survived throughout the entire classical, Hellenistic and Byzantine age until the appearance of the medieval castle.

Archaic inscription from Panayia Limnia.

During the period of the Persian Wars, in which so many ideas and concepts were put to the test in Greece, Skiathos was one of the few towns that did not give in and did not go over to the side of the enemy. In fact, during the third Persian campaign (480-479 BC) its harbour provided a base for the three triremes of the Hellenic outpost that monitored the movements of the Persian fleet as it sailed down from the Thermaic Gulf toward the strait of Euripus. Herodotus reported that in 480 BC, the Hellenes who were awaiting the Persian fleet at Artemisium at the northern tip of Euboea, were alerted to the Persians' arrival by the signal fires that had been lighted by the Skiathians. Herodotus also reported that on the west coast of Skiathos, the first act was played in the naval battle of Artemisium between the three triremes, one from Athens, one from Aegina and one from Troezene, and ten Persian scouting vessels. The Greek triremes were soundly defeated and Xerxes erected a pillar on the Myrmigas shoal in the Skiathos channel - the first structure built to identify a shoal - to alert ships to the danger and give them time to avoid running aground. However, the information obtained by the Hellenes from the Skiathians about the arrival of the Persians was decisive to the outcome of the naval battle of Artemisium, in which the Hellenes, under the command of the Athenian Themistocles and the Spartan Eurybiades, defeated the Persian fleet.

Classical - Hellenistic period

In 478 BC the First Athenian Confederation or Delian League, which had been organised to confront the Persian threat more effectively, welcomed Skiathos, with its independent and democratic political system, into its ranks. The cost of the Delian League and later the hegemony of Athens was covered by the League's tax which was paid by regions. As we are informed by Attic inscriptions, Skiathos was considered part of the region of Thrace for tax purposes, and contributed 1000 drachmas per year to the "Thrace tax". The fact that the island contributed money, in contrast to other cities which provided ships, and that this amount of money was small, leads to the conclusion that its economy was not particularly robust. This impression is reinforced if we take into account that the amount of the tax was determined in proportion to the annual revenue of each city. After the end of the Peloponnesian War (404 BC), and the victory of Sparta, Skiathos found itself under the latter's suzerainty and its political system became an oligarchy. After Conon's victory at Cnidus in 394 BC, the island once again acquired its freedom; later, under the peace of Andalcidas (386 BC), Skiathos became officially autonomous and independent.

But the Spartans failed to respect the treaty, and violated the peace by re-occupying Skiathos. The Skiathians in a short while threw off the Spartan yoke. With the help of the Athenian general Chabrias (378 BC) they formed an alliance with the Athenians - the Second Delian League - and established autonomy and peace for at least 40 years on their island. It was a period of prosperity for Skiathos and in fact during those years (mid-4th century BC) the island even minted its own bronze coins bearing the name CKIAΘI, on which was depicted the head of Kerdoos (Bringer of Gain) Hermes, protector of trade. During the latter years of this extremely productive period, the Athenian allies transformed Skiathos into their base of operations against Philip II of Macedonia. The Athenian orator Demosthenes insisted that Skiathos (together with Limnos and Thasos) were extremely important from a strategic point of view, which was why they had to be organised defensively in order to be used as an Athenian stronghold against Philip. The island also provided berths for ships and provisions for troops. Regarding this period, Demosthenes said that when Philip II captured Skiathos, he installed a pro-Macedonian tyrant on the island. The year 341 BC was when democracy returned to Skiathos. Then, the Athenian general Cephisophon liberated Euboea and Skiathos by means of a fleet and an army.

But the defeat of the Athenians at the battle of Chaeronea in 338 BC sealed the fate of Greece and signified the definitive end of independence for its southern section. The Macedonians triumphed everywhere, and Skiathos was no exception. After the death of Alexander the Great, there was a succession of masters on the Greek mainland. The island fell under the dominion of Antipatros, of Antigonos, of Demetrius the Polyorcetes (Besieger), and finally of the Romans. Skiathos suffered greatly in the war launched by Philip V of Macedonia against the Romans. At the beginning of the Second Macedonian War (200-199 BC), as the Roman historian Livy recounted, in order to prevent Skiathos and Skopelos from falling into the hands of the Romans, Philip V applied the scorched earth tactic and laid waste to both islands. In the same year, both the Roman fleet under admiral Lucius Apustius and the fleet of Attalus landed on devastated Skiathos. They grabbed whatever was left after the depradations of Philip. However, apart from the destruction of part of the wall and the looting, Skiathos was not levelled, which made possible its rapid reorganisation afterwards.

In 197 BC, after Philip was defeated at Cynoscephalae, Skiathos regained its democratic political system. In 192 BC, a new raid was conducted against the island, this time by Antiochus III of Syria, who seized the residents' entire grain crop and any other food that was found. Generally speaking, life on Skiathos at this period was especially turbulent with marked political shifts that not infrequently acted as a brake on the island's development.

Roman period

Meanwhile the Romans, taking advantage of the discord between the Greek city-states, proceeded to establish themselves on the conquered lands. Following the dissolution of the Macedonian state in 168 BC, they ceded some elementary liberties to the Skiathians after the congress of Amphipole. And when all of Greece passed into the hands of the Romans in 146 BC, Skiathos lived peacefully in its oblivion. In 88 BC, Mithridates VI, king of the Pontus, within the context of his war against the Romans, appeared as a liberator. He burned and laid waste the island, turning it into a launching point for his attacks as well as a storage place for his booty. But even after Mithridates' defeat, stability did not return to Skiathos. The permanent threat of pirates evolved into their undisputed domination over the Aegean Sea, despite the short-lived victory by Pompey (68-67 BC) who attempted to curb them.

After the battle of Philippi in 42 BC, the victor Mark Antony gave Skiathos to the Athenians in exchange for the friendship they offered him. The lovely island was turned into a place of exile, a hideout and base of operations for thieves and pirates.

Meanwhile, a new era had dawned in the world with the birth of Christ. Skiathos remained under the suzerainty of the Athenians for many years into the Christian era and in 193-221 AD it once again passed over to the Romans. This was during the reign of Septimius Severus during which the island was autonomous, with a Boule (council), an assembly of the Deme (town), and an Eponymous Archon (Designated Leader), as revealed by an inscription that can still be seen at the entrance of the Town Hall.

During the period of Roman rule, this town on the island of Skiathos had already begun to grow and to spread out beyond the walls, as revealed by traces of an aqueduct, Roman mosaics, reliefs and inscriptions dedicated to Hadrian and to Septimius Severus.

Christianity, the new religion, appeared on the island in 325 AD, and the island's first church was built in 530, and consecrated to the Holy Trinity.

On the road to Kastro.

Byzantine period

There is no information available about life in Skiathos during the early years of the Byzantine empire. What we do know is that it was then considered part of the Byzantine province of Thessaly and, like the other islands of the northern Sporades, constituted a part of the Macedonian Theme (with its capital in Thessaloniki) and had an bishop's see, which belonged to the Metropolis of Larissa. The Emperor Constantine VII Prophyrogenitus (913-959) in his work "Re: themes", which deals with the administrative division of the Byzantine empire into administrative units called themes, stated that Skiathos had a local leader. We also know the names of two bishops of Skiathos, Demetrius (early 6th century) and Straton (7th-8th century). Certain charges by Demetrius provided the grounds on which the Metropolitan Stephanos of Larissa was removed from office for irregularities by the Ecumenical

Patriarch Epiphanius. The building of the island's pier is attributed to Straton. When Bulgarians and Slavs attacked Thessaloniki in 758 AD during the reign of Constantine V Copronymus, the emperor who was engaged in the famous Iconoclastic controversy, the Byzantine fleet commanded by Sisinnius anchored in the Skiathos port in order to approach Thessaloniki.

In the 7th century, Saracen pirates started their devastating raids on the islands of the Aegean Sea. Their leader was Leon, admiral of the Emir of Crete, and Damianos, who made incursions upon Demetrias. It must be regarded as certain that Skiathos did not escape their plundering. The town may have been transferred from the port to northern Skiathos during the reign of emperor Nicephorus Botaniatis (1078-1081) for reasons of defence and safety from pirate raids. It was then that a new town was built in the fortified position "Kastro" or "Palaiokastro" (Old Castle) or "Horio", some ruins of which have been preserved.

Venetian rule

In 1204, after sacking Constantinople, the Crusaders established their rule over territories of the Byzantine Empire, including the Aegean islands and Skiathos, which they gave to the Venetians. Skiathos and Skopelos were occupied in 1207 by the Venetian brothers Andrea and Ieremia Ghisi, with the help of Marco Sanudo, administrator of the duchy of the Aegean who was based on the island of Naxos.
But entrepreneurs Andrea and Ieremia Ghisi had other ambitions. They won the loyalty of the Skiathians by giving them self-government and a good many privileges (referred to in the famous Capitula Sciati et Scopuli), and then set themselves up as rivals of the dukes of Naxos. During this early period of Venetian rule, the Orthodox bishopric was abolished. The Ghisi brothers built a new castle on Skiathos both as a residence for themselves, and to protect the

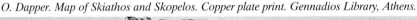

O. Dapper. Map of Skiathos and Skopelos. Copper plate print. Gennadios Library, Athens.

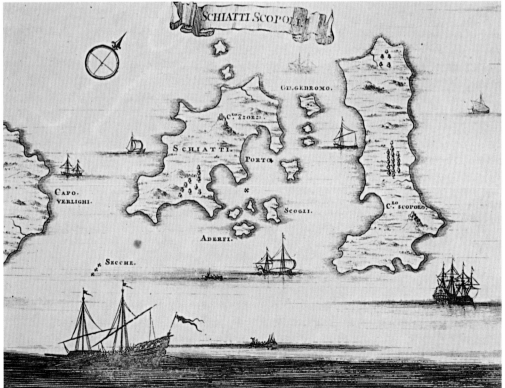

town. This castle is known today as Bourtzi, in the main port. Then it was called "Castello of St George", after the chapel situated on it. The Venetian lords remained on Skiathos for more than fifty years (until 1259). Their successors kept the island until 1276. Then Licarius, Italian admiral of the Byzantine emperor Michael VIII Palaeologus, chased the Venetians out of the Sporades and arrested Philippo Ghisi, one of the sternest and most arrogant leaders of his time.

Another version of the story has the move to the Kastro taking place during the period when Byzantine rule was reinstated on the island. The Byzantine central administration was then incapable of protecting its citizens against either pirate attacks or the conflicting designs of the Venetians, Genoans and Turks who kept quarrelling among themselves, culminating when the island once again fell into the hands of the Venetians. Papadiamantis reports characteristi- cally that the Kastro "can recount five centuries of harrowing history of suffering and blood."

Skiathos returned to Venetian rule, with minor interruptions, until the Fall of Constant- inople to the Turks in 1453. With the collapse of Byzantium, the Skiathians asked the Venetians to occupy their island instead of the Turks, in order to avoid the fate of the Imperial City, laying down terms including the privileges they'd been given during the Ghisi era, and that the Orthodox bishopric would remain on the island. The Venetians agreed and stayed on Skiathos, Skyros and Skopelos until 1538, with a short interruption between 1475-1486, when the islands were captured by the Turks during a Venetian-Turkish clash.

During this second period under the Serenissima, the Venetians proved to be unprincipled and unsympathetic tyrants.

Turkish rule - Liberation

In 1538, the terrible pirate Khayr-ad-Din Bar- barossa attacked and captured Skiathos after a six-day seige. It was then that the castle of Bourtzi was abandoned. In 1540, with the signing of the peace between Venice and Turkey, Skiathos was once again handed over to Turkey.

From a document in the Patriarchate of Constantinople, we learn that in 1576 Skiathos and Skopelos had a bishop, 50-60 priests and 2000 houses. In 1660, the Venetian admiral Francesco Morosini captured the Kastro and thus the island briefly came under Venetian rule again. But from the 18th century on, Skiathos was ruled by the Capudan Pasha, admiral of the Turkish fleet, and the dragomans. The Skiathians paid a poll tax and suffered, as did the other peoples under Turkish rule, from the measure of compulsory sea service in the Ottoman Empire's fleet under appalling conditions. Later, this measure was replaced by a tax called melahika (melah =seaman). At that period, a community institution came into being by which the notables or elders assisted the Turkish administrator, the voevod. Also, a cadis was appointed to handle judicial matters, an agas for administrative ones and an zambitis for tax issues. Gradually the administration of the island was assigned to the elders and to the Greek deputies of the Sultan, but always under the watchful eye of the central Ottoman administration. The Skiathian people were permitted to preserve their religious faith intact; after 1794 it was focused in the Monastery of Evangelistria. Schools were also run in the monasteries (at St John Parthenis and St John Kryfos) where educated monks taught. Meanwhile, pirates from Venice and Livorno and the Knights of St John, the latter Christians in other respects, continued their raids against Skiathos, devastating it and then leaving. In about 1790, refugees from Limni in Evia came to the island.

In the early years of the 19th century, the Skiathians began to develop another craft: ship building. In their shipyards (tarsanades) they began building boats large and small, destined for transportation and trade. They travelled to Egypt, to the shores of north Africa, and to destinations as far away as the Black Sea. Adamantios Korais wrote in his Statistics that Skiathos had 12 ships with 144 seamen and 48 cannons. Thus the War of Independence against the Ottomans in 1821 did not find them unprepared. The Skiathians had taken part in many uprisings and incursions against the Turks, under the Russian admiral Alexis Orlov in 1778-1788 in the victorious naval battle of Cesme, or under either Lambros Katsonis or the chieftain Nikotsaras in 1805 and 1807.

After the Orlov mutiny was stifled in 1770, the pre-revolutionary movement of armatoloi (local militias) and klefts (brigands) from Olympus continued in Skiathos and Skopelos, where they sought refuge between 1805 and 1816. With them, for a short period, was Theodore Kolokotronis, the well-known hero of the Greek War of Independence in 1821. All together they equipped a small fleet whose raids prepared the ground for the Revolution. Meanwhile, there were problems of shelter and food with the arrival on the island of 30,000 refugees from Epirus, Olympus, Pelion and Evia. But the time had come for the great struggle. Skiathos entered the Revolution under the leadership of, among others, the notables Alexandros Logothetis (great-grandfather of Papadiamantis) and Epipha-nios Dimitriadis, Skiathian teacher of the Nation. The Skiathians, stirred up by the members of the Philiki Etairia, entered the fight for freedom wholeheartedly. They fitted out their ships and took part in a good many raids. At the end of the War, the island became a refuge and launching base for pirates (Capodistrias suppressed piracy). The Protocol of the Independence of Greece which was signed in London in 1830 included Skiathos, Skopelos, Alonnisos and the surrounding uninhabited islands within the frontiers of a free and independent Greece. Freedom was a reality.

At this time, the Kastro, which then had 1500 inhabitants, was abandoned for good. The town in the port expanded day by day. The local people built homes on the seashore and in the interior towards Kalo Pigadi, to which they transported quantities of building material from the Kastro, hastening the ultimate desertion of the old town. The people from Limni who had sought refuge in Kastro in 1821, returned to the high ground of Aï Yiannaki and Plakes. This part of the town was called Limnia.

The Modern period

After liberation, shipping was resumed, and commercial sailing ships began being built again, using pinewood. The 1500 inhabitants of Skiathos had become 2000 by 1845. In 1855, the street plan of the town was initiated. A little earlier, Alexandros Papadiamantis was born on the island. By 1870 Skiathos had 2814 inhabitants who lived in 740 houses. In 1879, the number of residents had increased to 3084. Today the total population of the island exceeds 6000.

From the time of Otto, the first King of the Hellenes, until 1914, Skiathos was a municipality (deme). In 1914, it became a community which it remained until 1965, when it became a deme again. In 1897, during the Greek-Turkish war, the Greek fleet used the harbour of Skiathos as a base. During the national discord in 1917, Skiathos took sides with the Venizelos party and with the state in Thessaloniki, but not without local objections.

The Town of Skiathos was almost totally destroyed by German bombs during the Nazi occupation of Greece. On 14 September 1943, the Germans sank the submarine Katsonis seven miles off the coast of the Kastro in northern Skiathos, together with V. Laskos and his heroic crew. Also, on 23 August 1944, just before Greece's liberation, the Nazis burnt the island and executed seven Skiathians in reprisal for the capture by Resistance fighters of the German naval commander of the Northern Sporades. In these difficult years, the Kastro provided a refuge for British, Australians and New Zealanders. The local people would risk their lives to help allied soldiers hide and then escape. In this category of anonymous heroes was Kaliarina.

During the post-war period, the economic and social life of Skiathos developed rapidly with the help of active local authorities and of Skiathians everywhere, who never cease to be devoted to their little island.

CULTURE & TRADITION

People & Occupations - Customs & Manners
Architecture - Skiathos: Island of Scholars

Skiathos, the island of Alexandros Papadiamantis, is a singularly beautiful island in the northern Sporades. Its verdant greenery and lovely coasts justly attract many visitors every year who choose the island for their summer holidays. The culture of Skiathos plays a part in this choice. It is reflected in the faces of the inhabitants who welcome visitors to their island. This is why they do their best to make everybody's stay there as pleasant as possible. With this thought in mind, the Municipality of Skiathos organises a number of events each year under the general title of "Dream on the Waves" (Oneiro sto Kyma) to satisfy the cultural demands of both the local people and visitors to the island. In addition, the Papadiamantis Museum is open most of the day, and the exhibition put on by the Women's Association of Skiathos, which runs all summer long in municipal premises along the town's coast road, will be of interest to all those who appreciate folklore and traditional sweets.

Bust of Alexandros Papadiamantis
Right, the road to Kastro.

People & occupations

Of all the images of the island, it is likely to be the cordial and smiling Skiathians that you will remember most vividly. The relative prosperity experienced in recent years as a result of the growth of tourism has contributed to their kindness. Skiathians are no longer obliged to go elsewhere to make a living to feed their families, frequently working as ordinary seamen on ships built in their homeland. Today, the island has changed and the local people are imbued with this sense of change.

A large percentage of modern Skiathians live on their island and work in some sector of the island's marketable products such as oil, grapes, cereals, fruit and vegetables. Viticulture in particular has been highly developed on the island since ancient times. The dark red wine of Skiathos has always been among the best of its kind. Also known for their quality are the wine from the moschato variety of grapes, with its floral bouquet, and the alypiako, a wine famous for banishing sorrows.

Perhaps the only occupation in which Skiathians distinguished themselves in the past but has disappeared today is shipbuilding. Skiathians began practising this craft in 1829. The island has forests of wild pines, i.e. timber suitable for building ships. This era lasted until 1930 when Skiathian craftsmen and ships' carpenters were not building little boats but large commercial vessels. Its boatyards (tarsanades) were in operation from the end of the 18th century in the bay of Kechreas which was the shipyard of the Kastro.

Today the local people have given up this craft to take up tourism as their main occupation. The growth of tourism lent a significant thrust to the island and brought financial prosperity to its inhabitants, who today are enjoying a comfortable life. But memory frequently conjures up moments that have marked the history of the place. Someone sitting in the harbour looking at the rowboats and local caiques moored alongside yachts may call to mind the years when the Skiathian boatyards worked ceaselessly making the famous skaria that would sail as far as America: in Plakes, Zaharaki, Glyfoneri and Limanakia as far as St George's pond, when armies of ships' carpenters once created masterworks to sail the world's seas and oceans.

The once famous Skiathian tarsanades *(boatyards) are now a thing of the past.*

Customs and manners

The common feature of Skiathian customs and manners is the strong religious feeling which is expressed in all aspects of human activity. **Religious feasts** on Skiathos are very important events, the most significant being the Epitaph (Interment) of the Virgin at the monastery of Evangelistria celebrated on 15 August, and the procession in which the icon of the Panayia Kounistra, patron of the island, is carried from the town to the monastery of the same name, which is celebrated on the 21 November, the other major feast of the Virgin, the Presentation. The local people have made many praiseworthy efforts to preserve the Christian monuments in the Kastro and on the rest of their island, by dedicating their limited free time to repairing churches and monasteries that have been damaged by the ravages of time.

The history of the Monastery of Evangelistria (Virgin of the Annunciation) is as follows:

Skiathos was a place of refuge and an operations base for the famous armatoloi (local militias) of mainland Greece, among whom was the fearless leader Nikotsaras. Many of them would visit the monastery of Evangelistria to receive communion and confess to the priest Father Niphonas. In fact, some of them, upon the advice of the priest, would abandon the life of the klephts (brigands), marry and settle down, as the Christian way of life demanded. The leader, seeing the ranks of his army dwindling, decided that the priest had to die. But when he arrived on the threshold of the old man's cell and raised his sword to kill him, he saw the archangel Michael, followed by a bolt of lightening which blinded him. The priest, despite Nikotsaras' confession that he was about to kill him, blessed him and cured him.

According to tradition, the miraculous icon of the Virgin Kounistra was found in the following way: during the period of Turkish rule, a priest monk named Symeon saw a light

The traditional folk dance of Skiathos, called kamara.

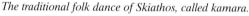

shining in the forest at night. He tried many times to find it, but each time the light would vanish. After much prayer and fasting, and with great persistence, he went back to the forest where he found the icon of the Virgin hanging in a tall pinetree. A young priest from the Kastro managed to bring it down from the tree, and on that site a monastery was built. Every year the monastery celebrates this event; the faithful gather on the previous day and keep a vigil in the courtyard around lighted bonfires. On the day of the feast they bear the icon in procession around the town. Indeed, the children used to believe that, when the icon of the Kounistra felt light in the monastery, it was from the pleasure of returning home, while on the contrary, when it was brought down to Hora, it felt heavy because it was sorry to leave its home. The procession of the icon was also held during the celebration of the finding of the icon, on the Sunday between 2 and 8 July. It is also said that in the Kastro, every old house had its zodio, a charm that took the form of a lucky animal which was slaughtered when its foundations were laid. If something bad was going to happen in the home, the animal would be heard moaning.

The island has many customs related to all the important events in religious and social life (marriage, death, birth, etc.), even to the well-being of the home.

The most characteristic customs, however, are those which constitute part of the **traditional Skiathian wedding**, such as the artifices used to prevent the bridal couple's enemies from "throwing girls at the bride", i.e. causing the bride not to give birth to male children: for example, the groom and bride put their shoes on a coin, or the groom puts sesame in his pockets to ward off the evil. The wedding feast is lavish and elaborate. Rice must be served, for the couple to "take root". The bride and groom are the first to dance, and then all the relatives and guests dance with the bride. Whoever leads the dance is obliged to give money to the musicians. The feasting goes on until morning.

Easter is also celebrated on Skiathos in a particularly festive spirit. Anyone who visits Skiathos at **Eastertime** will have an opportunity to enjoy many of the special sweets and foods prepared for the occasion including tsourvas (soup made of chopped lamb's entrails and rice), the Easter kouloura (which is round bread with a hole in the middle decorated with the traditional dyed red eggs), and the Easter kokona (dough figures of people or birds).

In the past, after the Ascension and after the feast of St George, the **"Kamara"** was danced, the characteristic **traditional dance** of Skiathos. The folk song of Kamara is a variation of the haunted bridge motif that can be found all over the country. It tells the tragic tale of a woman named Areti (Virtue), the wife of the master craftsman, who sacrifices herself and is buried alive in order to save the project.

The main feature of Skiathian feasts used to be the **local costumes**, which the islanders would wear with great pride on official feastdays.

The traditional outfit of Skiathian males stopped being worn in the 19th century, when it began to be replaced by European dress. For this reason, there are very few descriptions of it. In any event, it included breaches and a fesi (a cap of soft red felt) with a long tassel and showed similarities with the clothing worn by men of Hydra at the same period.

Traditional women's dress was richer in adornments and more valuable because of the embroidery, the fabric and the effort involved in making it. Skiathian women used to work for months or even years to make the clothing for their dowries. A good many examples of women's traditional dress have been preserved, which is why it can now be described in detail.

It consisted of a chemise or poukamiso (below knee-length, with long sleeves), a vest or fanela (crossed in front and fastened with two small buttons at the throat), stockings (when they are woollen, they are called tsourapia and come up to the knee), the gounaki (looks like a little shirt, is made of felt, has a knitted button at the throat and bears many woven decorations called armatosia on the sleeves and under the arms), the baboukli (resembles a short waistcoat with sleeves, made of velvet, closes with two small buttons under the bust, revealing the gold-embroidered neck of the chemise and bears many gold and silver-embroidered decorations on the bromanika, i.e. the inside bottom parts of the sleeves), the kouzouka (velvet waistcoat, open in front with decorations at the neck), the foustani or foustana (wool, silk or cloth dress), bell-shaped and pleated with a woven gold band sewn round the hem, the kolovoli (petticoat), the mallina (under-dress), the belt or zoni (always gold, it was tied over the baboukli and ended in two tsaprakia, i.e. incised silver or gilt clasps, sometimes inlaid with precious stones), the zonari (silk kerchief tied in front) and the boktsa (large woollen fringed kerchief which was worn in winter around the shoulders with the two ends crossed over the bust).

Traditional Skiathian women's dress.

This costume was accompanied by long earrings (sometimes with coins), bracelets, rings, pins and the koulaina, a gold chain necklace from which gold coins would hang.

Examples of traditional Skiathian dress can be seen on the Skiathos coast as part of the exhibition of the Women's Association. Throughout the summer in a small municipal garden, the Association displays various traditional objects such as household utensils, weavings, furniture from a traditional Skiathian home, etc. Visitors can also sample sweets, liqueurs and honey, all made of the purest ingredients. The sweet called aspro is made of almonds and sugar syrup, and is considered a "betrothal" sweetmeat; there is also marzipan, or amygdaloto, made of almonds and rosewater.

Skiathos, island of scholars

It was on this famous Greek island that Capodistrias opened the first upper School and an allilodidaktiko (mutual teaching) establishment on free Greek territory in 1828. This was the continuation of the school in the monastery of St John Parthenis that was mistakenly called Kryfos tou Eleimonos (Hidden monastery of the Benefactor) and founded in 1809. The scholar Epiphanios Dimitriadis was the principal of this school. Between 1835 and 1841, another school opened its doors to pupils from the island, financed by the inhabitants. This school later became a scholarcheio (a 3-form school for children aged 10-13) and functioned as such until 1929. It is worth pointing out here that it was hardly accidental that Skiathos became known as the "island of scholars", since there were always individuals and organisations such as the Association of Women of Skiathos, and cultural and athletic clubs etc. that contributed to the educational and cultural development of the island. The work of the Papadiamanteio-Moraitideio library has also been noteworthy. Its books and other publications, owing to lack of space, are being temporarily housed in the library of the Cultural Centre of Skiathos Churches.

Many inhabitants of the island have been engaged in letters, culture and science. From the pre-Papadiamantis era, we would note the name of Ananias who lived in the 18th century and became archbishop of Tzia (Kea) and Thermion in 1772, as well as Epiphanios Dimitriadis, a well-travelled man of letters, who wrote a paper in the 18th century that more or less predicted the invention of radio and television, and who was later appointed voevod of Liodromia by Ioannis Kallimachis. Included among the old scholars of Skiathos was Dionysios Epiphaniadis (1802-1882) who taught in Constantinople and in the Cyclades.

The secular monk Alexandros Papadiamantis

"Wherever evil finds you, my brothers, wherever your mind becomes dim, cite Dionysios Solomos and cite Alexandros Papadiamantis."

These spare, simple lines were written by the Nobel-prize winning Greek poet Odysseus Elytis in his Axion Esti to encourage the Greeks, to fortify their spirit, and to protect them from evil thoughts and deeds.

He reminded them that they should always remember Solomos and Papadiamantis because both give strength, courage and hope.

When one hears the name of Skiathos, immediately the name of Alexandros Papadia-mantis comes to mind. This is because Papadia-mantis, the great "saint" of Greek literature, was born on this island. He has been described as a great author, the most important writer of modern Greek short stories, a man whose entire life was a model for identifying the life and work of a great creator.

Alexandros Papadiamantis grew up in a poor, profoundly religious family, and from a very tender age followed his father, a priest, in his ministerings. He finished primary school on Skopelos; the remark noted in the school records about him was: "Graduated with highest honours". He went to high school in Halkida where he made his first literary efforts. He started third year of junior secondary school (then first year secondary school) at the Ionidio School in Piraeus but abandoned it in 1872 to become a monk on Mount Athos. He returned to Skiathos and then to Athens to attend the Varvakeio School. In 1874, he wrote his first poem dedicated to his mother. He finished the Varvakeio and registered in the Faculty of Philosophy at the University of Athens, which he was never able to finish, for reasons of poverty.

He taught himself English and French. In 1876, he lived in the poor Athens neighbourhood of Psyrri. In 1879, he wrote his first book I Metanastis ("The Migrant Woman"). It was followed by Embori ton Ethnon ("Merchants of the Nations") in 1884 and I Yiftopoula ("Gypsy Girl") in 1884. In the meantime, he had met V. Gavrielidis, the founder of professional journalism in Greece. Papadiamantis was given work on newspapers as a translator and then as a journalist, as his need to make a living was aggravated by his obligation under customary law of providing dowries for his three sisters. At this period, he contributed to the newspapers Asty, Akropolis, Mi Hanesai and Estia. Poverty accompanied him throughout his life. The story is told about the banker Andreas Syngros, who met Papadiamantis by chance at the Dexameni, and tossed him a penny believing him to be a beggar. Papadiamantis was by nature self-sufficient and content with little, and it is indicative of his modesty that he refused to accept the wage of 150 drachmas offered by Mr Kaklamanos, the editor of the newspaper Asty, replying with a characteristic phrase: "A hundred is enough for me." Because Papadiamantis' work would appear in the press in daily instalments, he never saw a single one of his books published. Even though his writing could have given him an opportunity to come into contact with literary circles in Athens (Palamas, Nirvanas, Malakasis, Vlachoyannis, and others), Papadiamantis avoided them because of his ascetic nature, preferring the company of ordinary people in coffee shops and tavernas. He and Moraïtidis used to chant in the chapel of Ayios Elissaios.

At the age of 30, he wrote letters to his parents giving the reasons for his lack of success. In March 1908, Papadiamantis left Athens for good, penniless, his fare paid by

Yiannis Vlachoyannis. After settling in Skiathos, he would send his work in to Athenian newspapers. He became seriously ill of bronchial pneumonia, and died on 3 January 1911, tended by his sisters.

He left behind an enormous and varied body of work which includes some 180 short stories, three historical novels, poems and countless translations, including works by Turgenev and Dostoyefsky (which he translated from French). The most important genre in his work is his short stories, which were collected together for the first time in a single edition in the mid-1950s by G. Valetas. Thematically they can be classified as follows: a) Skiathian stories, b) Athenian stories, c) festive stories (Christmas, New Years' etc.), d) nautical idylls and e) novellas. The two main sources of inspiration for Papadiamantis were Skiathos and the Orthodox Church.

The economy, the society, customs and manners, as well as the human characters on Skiathos are recorded with precision and elegance in his work. He has thus correctly been termed the greatest Greek observer of social behaviour.

But he did not remain confined by the narrow ethographic framework of his age.

His masterpiece, the novella I Fonissa ("The Murderess") is the best proof of his extraordinary ability to delve into the deepest recesses of the human heart and to dissect the social conditions in his homeland, deploring the injustice endured by females. The protagonist, an old woman named Frangoyannou, is among the most important in all of Greek literature.

Alexandros Moraïtidis

Another Alexandros from Skiathos, Alexandros Moraïtidis was Papadiamantis's cousin. He was born on the island in 1850 and also studied at the Faculty of Philosophy in Athens. In Athens he worked as a teacher and later on the newspapers Akropolis and Ephimeris as well as on many magazines in which he would publish travel articles containing his impressions of various regions of Greece that were still under Turkish rule. These impressions, his most important work, were published in six volumes under the general title: "On the waves of the North wind". He soon abandoned this profession and started working in journalism as an editor. He wrote many historical plays, comedies and church services, and translated many texts by the Fathers of the Church. His works are characterised by strong religious and patriotic feelings and a lyrical style. In 1920, Moraïtidis became a monk, took the name Andronikos and withdrew to Skiathos where he died on 25 October 1929. In the same year he was proclaimed member of the Academy of Athens, while previously, in 1921, he had received the National Award for letters and arts.

Bust of Alexandros Moraïtidis.

Architecture

The traditional architecture of Skiathos has been preserved in a small number of houses. The Skiathian house has three parts: the ground floor or katoï, the middle floor or sophas, and the upper floor. On the ground floor, wood was stored for the winter, barrels of wine were kept, as were earthenware jars containing oil and olives. The sophas was the apartment used as the family's main residence. This was a floor about 1-1.5 m. higher than the ground level, which you reached by walking up 4-5 steps, i.e. it was at a higher level covering part of the ground floor. The next floor was usually averto i.e. undivided. The entrance was by an external stone stairway or by an internal wooden staircase from the ground floor. At the top of the stairs, the landing was covered by a tabouk, or small wooden roof.

Many houses had enclosed verandahs which projected 30-40 cm out of the top floor on the side that looked out over the road, so that the area of the upper floor was larger than that of the ground

The architecture of Skiathos is simple and functional.

floor. This projection is a feature reminiscent of the architecture of Pelion. The roof or tsati of the Skiathian house also reminds us of Pelion and the Macedonian type, as it is covered with terracotta tiles or, in rarer instances, with slate tiles placed so that one overlaps the other.

Hora is densely populated and has graphic narrow streets paved with cobblestones. It is believed that this plan was first applied in the Kastro due to lack of space, and was applied in the new town out of habit. There are only a few Skiathian traditional houses that have a courtyard.

With respect to **ecclesiastical architecture**, most of the churches on Skiathos were built during the period of Turkish rule and up to 1850. Their construction followed the post-Byzantine or modern Greek tradition. The former, richer and more elaborate, came to Skiathos via Mount Athos and includes churches with wooden roofs with an aisleless nave (Christos in the Kastro, the Panayia Prekla) as well as a complex structure such as the Evangelistria Monastery. The technique of Byzantine ecclesiastical architecture was applied with precision. The second category of churches is in the plain folk style, using techniques from Mt Pelion, but it did not have much impact on the island. In this category are the two parish churches on Skiathos, the cathedral of the Three Bishops and the Birth of the Virgin (Panayia Limnia). Painted decoration has been preserved in just five churches (the church of Christos in the Kastro, the monastery churches of Panayia Kounistra, Ayios Ioannis Parthenis, and Panayia Kechria Evangelistria).

The walls of churches and monastery churches used to be adorned with plates (pinakia) that have been preserved in the katholika (main churches) of Kechria and Kounistra. These are ceramic plates from the town of Iznik in Asia Minor and from Italian workshops. They are placed in the dome and on the walls around the windows. The floors of the churches usually consist of large stone slabs without any particular ornamental design. The floor of the monastery church of Evangelistria is paved with decorative tiles from Italy.

Houses on Skiathos are reminiscent of the Mt Pelion style of architecture, while its churches show the architectural influence of Mt Athos.

Hora

The town of Skiathos has stood the test of time: it was the same town during the classical period, the same in the period of Alexander the Great, the same during the Roman and Byzantine periods. This same town managed to survive until the Middle Ages, at which time the population uprooted itself and moved to the Kastro.

But early in the 19th century, when the Skiathians abandoned the Kastro for good in 1829, they returned here again. The town became fairly densely populated, was razed to the ground by German bombs during the Occupation in World War II and was rebuilt after the war. Today the largest part of the island's population is concentrated here.

Skiathos town or Hora is built on the slopes of two low hills, at an altitude of just 20 m above sea level. The western side looks over the sea from a headland. Its centre is flat, and its eastern section is tucked under the hill of Ayios Nikolaos.

Skiathos has the traditional island architecture of a port town which has not been altered, despite the intense development of the past decade. A good many homes have balconies, covered verandahs, terracotta tile roofs, and some, albeit fewer, have flower-bedecked courtyards. Unfortunately, most of the old homes which resembled the mansions of Skopelos have been demolished, and in their place, new homes have been built. Few of the old ones have been preserved. After the Revolution of 1821, all houses were built in the rural style.

View of the town.

HORA & THE KASTRO

The main street, **Papadiamanti**, full of tourist offices and shops, restaurants and bars, cuts through Hora and ends at the port. The tiny, pine-covered **peninsula of Bourtzi** separates the commercial port from the old harbour where the fishing boats and caiques are moored. In the old days, there was a narrow inlet of water between the town and the fortress that is today covered by a wide road, making what had been an island into a peninsula. On this peninsula, the Ghisi brothers built a walled fortress with ramparts and loopholes called **Bourtzi** or the **Castle of St George** (from the little chapel of the same name inside it) both to protect the town and to use as their residence.

The Ghisi castle was destroyed in 1660 by Morosini. In 1906 Andreas Syngros had a primary school built on the site, which today houses the Cultural Centre and the Municipality's open air theatre, in which many cultural events are held.

Bourtzi:
graphic, everyday scenes.

In 1925, a bust of Alexandros Papadiamantis was put up in its entrance. A traditional coffee shop recently opened here in complete harmony with the green landscape. The **home of Alexandros Papadiamantis**, in which the author spent his childhood and was subsequently demolished, was located right opposite the existing structure. His family moved to the new house after the wedding of his older sister Urania, who received it as a dowry. This house has been transformed into a museum and includes many of the furnishings (bed, cask) and personal items (inkwell) that used to belong to the author. It is open from 09:30 - 13:00 and from 17:00 - 20:30 every day except Monday from April to October.

1, 2. *House and statue of Alexandros Papadiamantis.*
3. *Church of the Treis Ierarches (Three Bishops).*
4. *Panayia Limnia.*
5. *The Church of the Ayia Triada (Holy Trinity).*

3

In Pigadaki, to the left of the harbour is the Aï Yiannakis site (the church of St John of the Pier fell into the sea!).

Just below this site, there is a pier where the breakwater of the ancient port was located. Although very few traces of the pier remain, they represent a danger to large vessels. On a rock at one end there is an inscription from the year 900 AD:

"The most holy and blessed Straton built this jetty himself".

Among the churches in Hora, of particular interest is the **cathedral of the Three Bishops (Treis Ierarches)**, in which is the miraculous icon of the Panayia Eikonistria or Kounistra, part of the carved wooden icon screen of Panayia Prekla in the Kastro, and a large metal circle called a horos, bearing icons of the apostles and prophets under which medieval weddings were performed in the Kastro. In the Epano Yeitonia (Upper Neighbourhood), is the second parish church on the island, that of **Panayia Limnias or Apano Panayia** built in

4

1838 and dedicated to the birth of the Virgin. Papadiamantis' skull has been preserved in its narthex, together with some old icons from the churches of Christos and St Nicholas in the Kastro. Panayia Limnia took its name from the town of Limni on Evia. Refugees from Limni came to Skiathos in waves (1790, 1821, 1823) intermarried with the local residents and now, together, they constitute the population of the present town of Skiathos. A few steps farther on, marble blocks have been preserved from the wall of the ancient

5

town and nearby are traces of an early Christian basilica. During antiquity, the town was surrounded by a stout wall, sections of which can still be seen today. In the cemetery or Nekrotapheio area, beside the ruins of the ancient wall, and under the **church of the Holy Trinity (Ayia Triada)** are the vestiges of an older Christian church. Inside the town cemetery, to the left of the entrance, the two famous Alexanders of Skiathos are buried side by side.

On one of the three peaks of Hora's rocky hill is the **church of Ayios Nikolaos** on which is a clock installed in 1954. The icon of the Panayia Megalomata was brought here from the church of Panayia Prekla in the Kastro. One can enjoy a panoramic view of the town from the churchyard.

On the other peak stands a windmill which operates as a restaurant with "sails" built not of cloth but of thin boards. Near the port, on the coast at Tsiferi, is the last shipyard that builds, maintains and repairs the islanders' many small and large boats. During the summer months (June to September) a pavilion in the old harbour houses the folk art collection of the Association of Women of Skiathos, in which traditional handicraft goods are exhibited, as well as furniture, traditional dress, etc. In the courtyard of the Skiathos Military Academy one can still see the stone drums from the column built by Xerxes on the Myrmigas shoal in the Skiathos channel to warn ships of the danger of shipwreck. Farther along is the airport runway.

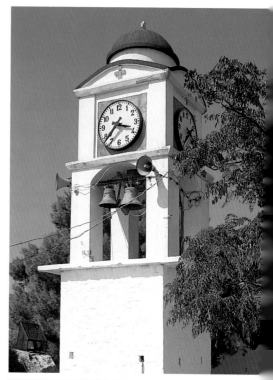

*Views of Hora
and the church of Ayios Nikolaos.*

Near the town, there are beaches suitable for swimming on Bourtzi, at **Plakes**, Kohyli and at the long beach of Megali Ammos. Caiques based in the port take visitors on tours round the island or to one of the many beaches. Caiques also make daily trips to the lovely little island of **Tsougrias**.

During the summer months, Hora assumes a cosmopolitan character, and it is then that many cultural events take place on the island. Every two years, boating competitions are held within the framework of Nautical Week. On 14 September, a celebration called Katsonia takes place in homage to the submarine Katsonis that was sunk by the Germans in 1943 in the sea off the Kastro. The most important of the religious feasts are the Epitaph of the Virgin at the monastery of Evangelistria on 15 August and the procession of the Panayia Kounistra icon from the town to the monastery of the same name on 21 November.

The beaches at Plakes and Tsougria are small but beautiful.

The Kastro

The easiest access to the Kastro (or Castle) on the north coast of Skiathos is by caique from the town or from Koukounaries or from anywhere on the northern coast. If you are driving, take the left turn before the monastery of Evangelistria, through a scenic area strewn with monasteries, follow the signs informing you where to leave your car, and then continue on foot until you arrive at an area with many shops. Images from the past life of the island, real and imaginery, fill the imagination of the visitor. Historically the Kastro is the most important site on the island. The medieval town was situated on a crag high up among the eagles' nests. Local and foreign visitors alike feel the need to climb up and pay their respects to the churches of Christos and Vangelistra.

The Kastro stands high up on a giant rock pounded by the waves of the sea. In the past this place was virtually impregnable. It was established in about the mid-14th century when the area was afflicted by the raids of Saracens and other pirates, at which time the Skiathians abandoned their town on the coast and came up here to protect themselves. The inhabitants of the Kastro were very few then. Their tiny dark houses were built side by side. Life was difficult because space was limited and there was a permanent fear of attack by pirates.

We can get an idea of this from an appeal written by the Skiathians to the supplier of the Venetian fleet on 8 November 1531, complaining that they were in danger of starving to death, because they could not cultivate their lands for fear of pirates. It was not until 1829 that the inhabitants of the Kastro abandoned it for good and went back to the main port.

The Kastro is a naturally fortified steep rock washed on three sides by the sea. On the side

A trip to Kastro is a pilgrimage to the beauty of nature and the splendour of the gods.

closest to the land there was a stout wall with ramparts and loopholes, part of which has been saved. The wall near the sea was not as strong.

The Kastro towers above a rough sea. A wooden drawbridge connected the fortress with the land. Today concrete stairs lead to the fortress gate. In front of it there was a colonnade, over which was a small tower and a "terrace" with loopholes and a zematistra (a protrusion from which boiling water or oil could be poured on attackers). The 300 houses, 22 churches and walls, apart from a small section, have all been destroyed. On the highland Barberaki, the cannon of Anangias has been saved. Trees have sprouted everywhere. Of the churches, only the churches of Christos, Ayios Nikolaos and Ayia Marina have been saved. The church of Christos, the post-Byzantine cathedral in the Kastro, is near the Panayia Prekla. It is an aisleless basilica with gabled roof.

The marble lintel on the gate refers to a remodelling in 1619. The templon (icon screen) and icons belong to the 17th century. The church's wood carvings and wall paintings are rare works of art, while the icon of Christ has the date 1652 inscribed on it. From the ceiling hangs the horos a large circle of metal adorned with the icons of saints, under which the inhabitants' weddings used to be performed.

On the ridge opposite, near the chapel of the Beheading of John the Baptist, was the cemetery of the medieval town. Under the Kastro there is a lovely beach, on which a little taverna operates during the summer months.

1, 2. The church of Christos and its interior.
3. Ruins of the church of Panayia Vangelistria.

On the other side of the rock, on the coast of Chaeremonas, once stood the oldest monastery on the island, now the ruins of what used to be the lovely church of Panayia Vangelistria.

Pyrgi sounded the warning to the Kastro. At Ayia Anastasia there are vestiges of the ancient Greek watchtower, although tradition argues that they were the homes of the Kastro dwellers who sought refuge there for a while after an attack by the terrible pirate Barbarossa.

The Kastronisia islands and the Kastro shore.

We have divided our tour of Skiathos into three itineraries so as to make every visitor's trip to the island as full and enjoyable as possible.

There are, it might be said, four roads that go round the island. One, the main road, starts out from the town and, following the southwestern coast, goes as far as Koukounaries, Ayia Eleni and Krassas. A second road starts at Troulos, before Koukounaries and, cutting across the island, arrives at its northwestern coast, at the Aselinos beach. And finally, a third road starts from the town and then, at a fork in the road, goes off in one direction toward Imeri Elia and in the other to the Monastery of Evangelistria.

But to have an overall picture of the island, in addition to the itineraries proposed, one can follow others according to one's instincts and moods. Starting from the Kastro and heading northwest, a fascinating coastline unfolds with beaches and caves. Small motorboats make trips to these caves on the north coast of Skiathos, as there is no way to get there by road. Skotini Spilia (Dark Cave), Galazia Spilia (Blue Cave), Trypia Petra (literally: The Rock with the hole in it), and the Lalaria beach await those who are lucky enough to be able to follow another, equally beautiful, route in a caique. For sports lovers, however, southern Skiathos usually has calm waters and is suitable for waterskiing while the northeastern and northwestern coasts, owing to the prevailing winds, are more suitable for wind surfing. And finally, the interior of the island is ideal for hikers and walkers because of its healthy climate and rich vegetation.

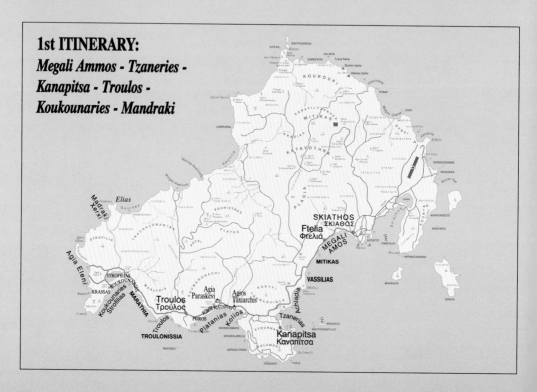

1st ITINERARY:

Megali Ammos - Tzaneries -
Kanapitsa - Troulos -
Koukounaries - Mandraki

THE ISLAND

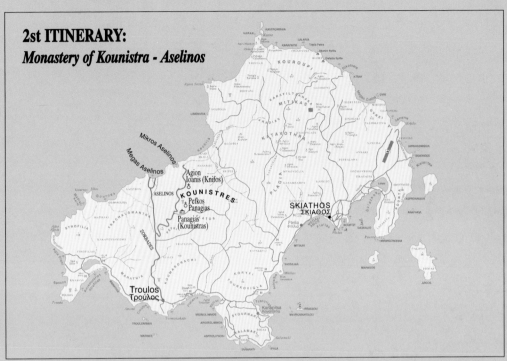

2st ITINERARY:
Monastery of Kounistra - Aselinos

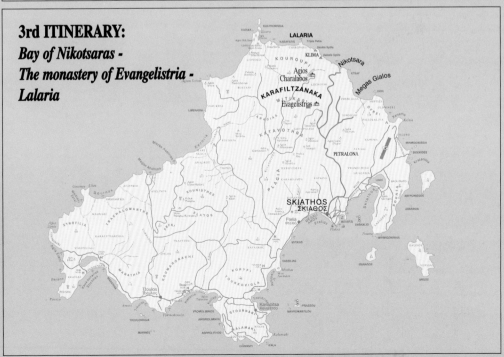

3rd ITINERARY:
Bay of Nikotsaras -
The monastery of Evangelistria -
Lalaria

1st ITINERARY:

Megali Ammos - Tzaneries - Kanapitsa - Troulos - Koukounaries - Mandraki

Starting out from the town, we drive in a southeasterly direction until we arrive at Koukounaries. The road runs along the seashore in a region full of hotels, sandy beaches with umbrellas, and tourist facilities of all kinds. Graphic coastlines, steeply walled bays and wonderful sandy beaches are the main types of scenery on this route.

As we turn into the bay of Ftelia, we enter the developed tourist region of **Megali Ammos**, with many hotels and inns. Here is historic Ftelia, where on 9 October 1823, Old Man Karatassos killed 400 Turks when the admiral Pasha Topal attacked the chieftains of Olympus. After Ftelia are the tourist areas of **Mytikas**, **Vasilias** *(3 km)*, the **Bay of Achladia** and **Tzaneries**.

*Megali Ammos with its beach,
and below, the beach named Vasilias.*

The **Achladia** beach is about 2.5 km from the town, and can be reached either by caique or by bus.

The coast is suitable for waterskiing and wind surfing. Also suitable for sea sports is **Tzaneries**, the beach ordinarily used by guests at the Nostos Hotel.

1, 2. Tzaneries.
3, 4. Achladia.

Ahead we can see **Kanapitsa** (6.5 km), and the peninsula of the same name, on which lovely country residences have been built. From Kanapitsa there is a secondary road which goes round the peninsula and reconnects with the main road three kms later. The lush green peninsula of Kanapitsa has hotels, villas and sandy beaches. It also has a diving school. The main road continues along the bay of Kalamaki-Vromolimnos, past the beaches of **Kolios** (ideal for sea sports), **Vromolimnos** (7 km) with its tavernas and sports facilities (schools for water-skiing, jet-skiing, water scooters etc), and the beaches of **Platania** and **Poros**, where one can find large hotels and organised beach facilities.

Beautiful Skiathian beaches.
1, 3. Kanapitsa.
2. Kolios.
4, 5. Vromolimnos.

Platania and Kolios.

1

2

3   On the Platania beach (8 km) is the **church of Aï Taxiarchis** and a little farther along, the church of Ayia Paraskevi, where a traditional fair is held on 26 June. The ravines in the region are a stopping point for rare migratory birds.

    The road arrives at **Troulos** (9 km) on the bay of the same name, with the **Troulonisia** opposite. Traces can be found here of the monastery "tou Theou Sofia" (or Divine Wisdom), dating from the reign of the Byzantine emperor Justinian, which burned down during the period of Frankish rule. On the site where the marina and its yachts are located today, the local people once fished for mullet, a fact reported by Athenaeus in his work Deipnosophistai, because mullet were a choice delicacy on the dining tables of the ancients.

1, 4. Troulos.
2. Platania.
3. The chapel of Ayios Taxiarchis.

We continue driving along Skiathos' main road. After the Marathon beach, we arrive at **Koukounaries** (13 km from the town), a wonderful site, perfect for cosmopolitan tastes, with many hotels, shops, restaurants, discos, bars, marinas and organised camping facilities. The fragrant forest of pine trees (koukounaries) has given the region its name.

But the biggest attraction of the region is its long sandy beach, which has been described as the most unspoiled natural beach in the Mediterranean. The road goes round the natural habitat of the **Strofylia pond** and comes back to Koukounaries. The beach is protected and has been developed for ecotourism with cofinancing by the Municipality and the European Union as an organisation model.

The ancient settlement at Koukounaries was **Kephalopoula**, famous for its transit trade. On the feast of St George, riding competitions are held at Koukounaries.

Koukounaries: one of the great beauties of nature on Skiathos.

1

2

There are two roads out of Koukounaries, one leading to the isolated sandy beach of **Ayia Eleni** (14 km) and the other to the **Krassas beach** (Banana). Ayia Eleni is situated opposite the southern shores of Pelion, offers good fishing and is famed for its spectacular sunsets. Krassas is a perfect beach for sea sports.

At the top of the hill overlooking the beach are the sparse ruins of a tower from which, according to Herodotus, a message was sent in 480 BC by phryktoria (a long-distance method of communication using lighted fires or torches), warning that the Persian fleet had sailed out of Thessaloniki.

On the northwestern coast, near Koukounaries, is the isolated **Mandraki bay** or **"Harbour of Xerxes"** from which Xerxes started out for the famous naval battle at Artemisium. It is an hour from Koukounaries

1. *The beach of Ayia Eleni.*
2. *The bay of Krassas.*
3. *Mandraki or Xerxes' Harbour.*
4. *Banana beach, ideal for lovers of sea sports.*

on foot. Mandraki, a narrow, one might even say virgin, stretch of coastline, offers wonderful scenery. Then we come to the equally isolated beach of **Elia**.

2nd ITINERARY:
Monastery of Virgin Kounistra - Aselinos

On this itinerary, starting out from Troulos, one can visit the post-Byzantine monasteries that kept the religious and cultural identity of the island alive during difficult times; it ends at the Megali Aselinos beach where the green of the mountain meets the azure of the Aegean.

*One road out of Troulos leads to **Zorbades**, where the Skiathos riding club is located, with its horses and ponies. From there it continues either toward the post-Byzantine **monastery of the Panayia Kounistra** or toward the organised beach of Megali Aselinos. The monastery of Panayia Kounistra is dedicated to the Presentation of the Virgin. Here the icon of the Virgin was once kept that can now be seen in the island's Cathedral.*

*Beside the church of the Panayia is the region called **Pefko tis Panayias** (Virgin's Pinetree), where, according to tradition, the icon of the Virgin was hanging from a tree (kounistra= swinging). Panayia Kounistra is the patron of the island and on her feast day, the Presentation of the Virgin on 21 November, there is always a great celebration. The Monastery was built in 1655. At that time, a Skiathian named Symeon was a monk in a little monastery. He found the icon of the Virgin and placed it in the monastery which gradually expanded as the fame of the miraculous icon spread. After this, the monastery was named "Kounistra". Another explanation of the name could be that the region is called Kounistres because the wind is almost always blowing here, owing to the altitude, causing the forest to rustle and move.*

1, 2, 4. The famous church of Panayia Kounistra.
3. The Panayia's pine tree.
5. The chapel of Timios Stavros.

2

3

4

5

Another possible explanation of the name of the monastery comes from the various traditions about the miraculous icon. According to one of these, the icon was found hanging from a tree where it was swinging in the air or shining like a star and this was why it was called Eikon Astria (which became corrupted into konistria), or according to another version, it came to Skiathos from Istria in former Yugoslavia. The monastery is equipped with loopholes for better protection from pirates. In 1726, its church was refurbished. In 1806 it became stavropigiako, or answerable directly to the Patriarchate in Constantinople. It was closed during the years of the Regency but in 1841, the monk Dionysios Gerontas renovated it completely. The church is a domed, aisleless basilica. The wall paintings in the church date from two different periods, from 1741 and 1805. The church's icon screen is of gilded, carved wood.

A little past the monastery of Kounistra, heading northward to the foot of the Kounistres mountain, is the post-Byzantine **monastery** called **Prodromos tou Partheni** (Precursor of Parthenios) which was founded in the 17th century. Its founder

4

was a Skiathian monk named Parthenios.
The katholikon or main church, restored in 1714,
is an aisleless basilica with a gabled roof. Its wall
paintings were remarkable, and the oldest of the
icons on the templon is that of Christ. This
monastery ran the first school on Skiathos when
the island was under Turkish rule. The *"Daskaleio"*,
the building in which the pupils lived, is today half
in ruins. One section of the cells was restored in
1895 by Alexandros Moraïtidis. The second
school that operated during the period of Turkish
rule was built on what are today the ruins of the
**monastery of Ayios Ioannis Paschalatos or
Kryfos** (St John the Hidden), on the other side of
the Kounistra mountain. From Zorbades, the road
takes us to the organised facilities of the **Megali
Aselinos beach** (14 km) where the mountain
meets the vast blue Aegean Sea. Aselinos has a
taverna, a covered parking and camping area,
and is suitable for windsurfing.

1, 2, 3. *Views of the interior and exterior*
    of Ayios Ioannis Kryfos.
4, 5. *The beach of Megali Aselinos.*

5

3rd ITINERARY:
Bay of Nikotsaras - The monastery of Evangelistria - Lalaria

From the town a road leads north toward the monastery of Evangelistria under the peak of Mt Karafiltzanaka. How one gets to the monastery depends on how much time one has available. It takes an hour to get there on foot from the town, up a fairly steep hill; it takes 20 minutes to drive up. After the Monstery of Evangelistria, the monastery of Ayios Haralambos and the post-Byzantine monastery of the Dormition (Kimisi) of the Virgin will be the next stops on our tour.

We pass through **Petralono** and the **Deserted Village** (Erimo Horio). It is believed possible that the second ancient town on the island was located here. The first detour of the road to the right leads to **Megas Yialos**, and a second road to the little inlet of Lechouni, which is today called the **Bay of Nikotsaras, or Harbour of Nikotsaras** where the chieftan Nikotsaras's comrades buried him after his death at Litohoro in 1808.

In the ravine of Agalianos once stood the **monastery of the Annunciation of the Virgin** (Evangelismos tis Theotokou). In 1794, Niphon, the priest-monk served at the monastery. Together with other monks, beside the ruins of the monastery of the Evangelismos, Niphon built the new post-Byzantine coenobite **monastery of Evangelistria**, the only monastery on the island that is currently functioning. In 1797 Constantine Handzeris, Dragoman of the Turkish fleet, showed interest in the monastery, and after that it became stavropigiako and by 1806, the works were completed and the monastery was renamed Nea Moni (New Monastery).

For a long period of time in the pre-revolutionary years, as we are told by the historian I. Frankoulas, the Monastery of Evangelistria concealed and gave shelter to armatoloi and klefts (warriors fighting for the liberation of Greece from the Ottoman Empire) from the rest of Greece who sought refuge on Skiathos. Here in September 1807, the oath of freedom was first made by revolutionaries and members of the Philiki Etaireia (Friendly Society). Here many captains made their oaths, including Yannis Stathas, Nikotsaras, and the great leader of the Revolution Theodore Kolokotronis.

1. Nikotsaras bay.
2, 3. Views of the monastery of Evangelistria.

Here the first Greek flag was made, with the colours of the army that are still in use today, i.e. a white cross on an azure blue ground; it was blessed by Nyphon. This monastery often assisted poor families of the island, although it too suffered from Turkish-Albanian pirates and thieves. Its decline began from 1850 on, as the number of monks diminished.

The monastery, although impressively large, cannot be seen from any distant point owing to the nature of the site on which it was built. The katholikon, which belongs to the Mt Athos Byzantine order, is a cruciform triconch church with three domes and two narthexes, a lite (inner narthex) and an exonarthex. Only in the sanctuary have a few wall paintings from 1822 been preserved and a magnificent carved wood icon screen outstanding for its rich decoration and fine representations. The floor is laid with plaques from Malta and faience tiles. The Evangelistria has three chapels: Ayios Dimitrios, the Timios Prodromos (St John the Baptist) and Zoodochos Pigi (Fount of Life). The first is housed in a strong, tall square tower pierced by loopholes; the second between the wings containing the cells, and the third is outside the churchyard, in the monastery cemetery. Initially the monastery had 65 cells, a kitchen, ovens, a common refectory, storerooms, stable, library, infirmary, and olive press. Many of these have been repaired and the effort

The dungeon in which Theofilos Kaïris was imprisoned.

continues. The library, which houses important books and documents, and the museum containing the relic (tibia) of Ayios Constantinos of Hydra (martyred during Ottoman rule), post-Byzantine icons, sacred vessels, glass and porcelain objects, are being refurbished. Another feature preserved at Evangelistra is the dungeon, in which the great teacher of the Nation, philosopher and cleric Theophilos Kaïris was imprisoned for five months, having been convicted of heresy by the Holy Synod in October 1839. On August 15, the Epitaph (Interment) of the Virgin is celebrated with great ceremony at this historic monastery.

A steep upward path leads from the Monastery of Evangelistria to that of **Ayios Haralambos** on Mt Kouroupi. Its date of construction is unknown. We do know, however, that it was renovated in 1809 and collapsed in 1834. In this aisleless, domed basilica, just one wall painting has been preserved, which is that of the Pantokrator on the dome. The icons on the templon are dated 1823.

East of Mt Karafiltzanaka, near the region of Kechrea, is the **chapel of Neos Apostolos** and the lovely post-Byzantine **monastery of the Dormition of the Virgin**, built in the Mt Athos style in 1540. It could be the destination of one of the most interesting excursions on Skiathos. It is 8 km. from the town. The monastery was restored in 1738 but unfortunately collapsed early in the 19th century. Although the monastery is closed, its aisleless cruciform triconch main church has been preserved, together with some of the wall paintings from 1745, some remarkable icons on the carved wood templon (18th century), two cells and the fountain inscribed with the year 1727.

Lower down in a prominent position is the **chapel of Panayia Katevodotras** containing three superb portable icons dated 1752 and 1779, and the fountains of Doman and Chaeremon.

From the port of Skiathos, one can visit the Lalaria beach by boat. This is a beautiful place with huge, steep rocky masses rising out of the sea. To the left there is is a large rock called Trypia Petra that creates a natural bridge between land and sea; before **Lalaria**, the **Blue** and **Dark Caves** compete for the visitor's attention.

Lalaria: where nature meets the gods (p. 71, 72-73).

6 SKOPELOS

Situated between Skiathos and Alonnisos, this island in the northern Sporades impresses the visitor from the very first moment. Dense pine forests cascade down from the peaks of the mountains to the delicate lace fringe of the coastline lapped by the blue sea. These steep shores on the island's north coast, with their impressive rock formations, create a bay in the northwest, the largest on the island. The first settlement on Skopelos, called Peparithos in antiquity, was built on this bay by the mythical Staphylos, son of Dionysos and Ariadne.

hades of pine and sea

Today the island's harbour is situated on this site, together with the charming town of Skopelos, clinging to the side of a steep hill and creating a picture of unique charm.

In contrast to the north coast of the island, the south and west coasts are calmer. Here the bays may not be as large as that of the port of Skopelos, but there are many of them and they are idyllic, with their calm crystalline waters, pine trees bending over the sea, and famous sandy beaches. Most of the villages on Skopelos are here, enveloped in green forest.

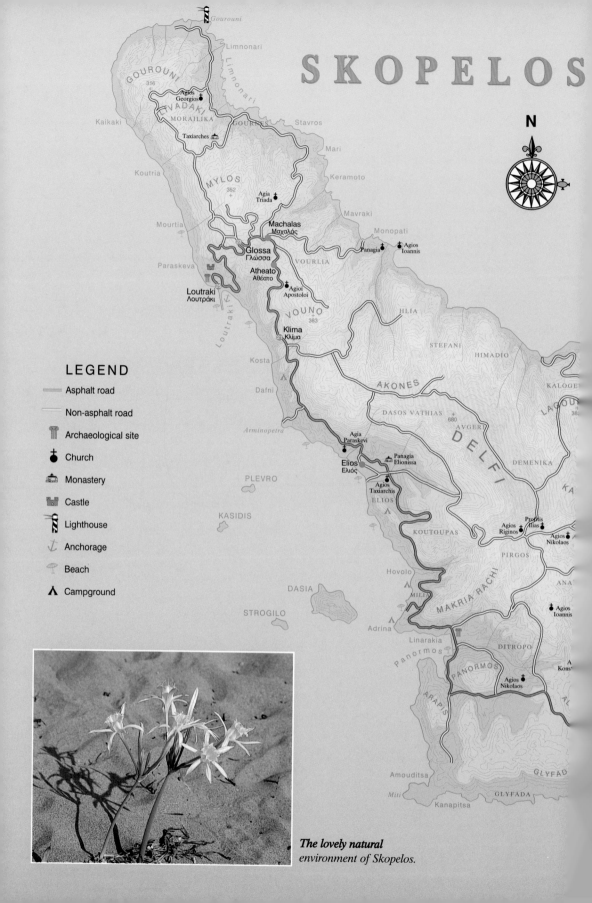

SKOPELOS

N

LEGEND

Asphalt road

Non-asphalt road

Archaeological site

Church

Monastery

Castle

Lighthouse

Anchorage

Beach

Campground

Gourouni

Limnonari

GOUROUNI
316

Agios
Georgios

EVADAKI

MORAILIKA

Kaikaki

GOURNES

Stavros

Taxiarches

Mari

Koutria

MYLOS
352

Keramoto

Mourtia

Agia
Triada

Mavraki

Machalas
Μαχαλάς

Monopati

Paraskeva

Glossa
Γλώσσα

Panagia

Agios
Ioannis

Atheato
Αθέατο

VOURLIA

Loutraki
Λουτράκι

Agioi
Apostoloi

VOUNO
383

HLIA

Loutraki

Klima
Κλίμα

STEFANI

HIMADIO

Kosta

KALOGE

Dafni

AKONES

LAGOU
38

DASOS VATHIAS
680

PLEVRO

Arminopetra

AVGER

DELFI

DEMENIKA

KASIDIS

Agia
Paraskevi

Panagia
Elionissa

Elios
Ελιός

KA

Agios
Taxiarchis

ELIOS

KOUTOUPAS

Agios
Riginos

Profitis
Ilias

Agios
Nikolaos

PIRGOS

STROGILO

DASIA

Hovolo

MILI

ANA

Agios
Ioannis

MAKRIA RACHI

Adrina

Linarakia

DITROPO

Panormos

PANORMOS

A
Kons

ARAPIS

Agios
Nikolaos

AL

Amouditsa

GLYFAD

Miti

GLYFADA

Kanapitsa

*The lovely natural
environment of Skopelos.*

Geography

Second largest of the Northern Sporades islands, Skopelos covers an area of 96 square kilometres, with 67 kilometres of coastline. Its highest mountain, Delphi (680 m.) is almost exactly in the centre of the island, with another peak, Palouki (566 m.) to the east. Between the two mountains the island narrows, forming the bay of Skopelos town to the north and that of Agnondas to the south. Skopelos has 4,700 inhabitants, employed chiefly in agriculture and during the summer months in tourism. Despite the fact that in recent years there has been an increase in tourism which undoubtedly constitutes an important source of revenue, it would not be true to say that tourist development is anything like an end in itself for the inhabitants of Skopelos. One proof of this is the fact that a considerable number of young people continue to prefer seafaring and farming occupations, in accordance with the local tradition. Skopelos has been famous since ancient times for the quality of its wine. According to tradition, Staphylos, the first settler on the island, discovered the grapevine and was the first to cultivate a vineyard. Today Skopelos is also famous for its plums which are reputed to be the best in the world. Generally, the island offers a great variety of vegetation. Plane trees nestle in the ravines that descend f rom the higher ground and in some places, olive trees give way to pines. Wherever there is a clearing, it is filled with vines, as well as almond, plum and other fruit trees.

Myth and history

Skopelos seems have been inhabited since the Neolithic era, given that on neighbouring Alonnisos, which is farther away from the coast of the central Greek mainland, there have been finds dating from that time. According to legend, the island's first settler was Staphylos, son of Dionysos and Ariadne.

The myth starts when Theseus, son of King Aegeus of Athens, left for Crete and killed the fearsome Minotaur inside the labyrinth of the palace at Knossos with the help of Minos's daughter Ariadne. Theseus took Ariadne with him on the return journey to Athens, but abandoned her on Naxos. The king of this island was Dionysos, who fell in love with her and had four children by her: Thoad, king of Limnos, Oenopion, king of Chios, Staphylos and Peparithos. The latter two were to play an important role in the history of Skopelos. They were both heroes. But in the myth there is a strange predilection for Staphylos, who is considered to have been the first settler and king of the island. One version says that he was Minos's Cretan general and that it was he who built the ancient town and planted the first vines and the first olive trees on the island. From that point on, grapevines and olive trees were grown on the island and became renowned for their quality. In addition, the word Staphylos and the Greek word staphyli (grape) have the same root. The admiration and affection for Staphylos went on for centuries, continuing into classical times, when the island's coins have a representation of Dionysos on one side and Staphylos on the other. In antiquity, however, the name used for the island was that of Staphylos's brother, Peparithos. The island was called Peparithos until the 2nd century AD, when Ptolemy the Geographer refers to it for the first time by the name Skopelos, obviously from the reefs (skopeloi in Greek) around it. Staphylos would have to be content with giving his name to the beautiful sandy beach on the south side of Skiathos where, according to legend, he disembarked with his Cretan comrades,

setting foot on the island for the first time.

But fate was ultimately to link myth to reality, and it is indeed rare for the connection to be so vital, so tangible. It was there, on Staphylos beach, that tell-tale traces were found, causing archaeological excavations to get under way in 1927; they concluded in 1936 with astonishing results. An ancient tomb, which contained impressive findings such as a gold sceptre, a sword hilt embellished with gold, gold jewellery, silver and stone vases, seal stones, bronze vessels, etc, was discovered intact. The gold sceptre can now be seen in the Archaeological Museum of Volos and the sword hilt is in the Archaeological Museum of Athens. There is no doubt that a tomb so rich in funeral gifts, and especially gold, must have belonged to an important person of those times, perhaps to a king. Who could it have been other than Staphylos?

Years went by after the colonisation of Peparithos by the Cretans. Here mythology intervenes again. The claim is that the island was conquered by Pelias, the king of Iolkos, near present-day Volos. It was Pelias who feared that his nephew Jason might one day take the throne from him so, in order to get rid of him, Pelias dispatched him to distant Colchis to bring back the Golden Fleece, hoping that he would die in the attempt. Even this myth could have some basis in historical fact because Iolkos is in the vicinity of the Northern Sporades islands, although the reference is probably to later events which occurred at the end of the Mycenean period.

After the Mycenean period, the island was captured by the Dolopians, a rough warlike people from Thessaly, who for many centuries used Skopelos as a base from which to launch their military operations. There is much justification for describing the colonisation of the island by Chalcidians in the 8th century BC as a deliverance from the tyranny of the Dolopians.

The Chalcidians founded three colonies: Panormos, Selinous and Peparithos, the latter of which they re-established. Coming from a city with seafaring traditions and experience in trade and transportation, the new settlers worked together with the longer established inhabitants with the result that Skopelos enjoyed a period of prosperity. Its ships took part in the transit trade, travelling as far afield as Chalcidice, Lesbos, Kos and even Sicily. It was at this time that silver coins were minted, gifts were offered by the islanders at the sanctuary of Delphi, and in 569 BC the runner Agnonas won a race at Olympia. To honour him, his fellow-citizens gave his name to the celebrated bay of Agnondas off the south coast of the island.

The prevailing peace was shattered at the beginning of the 5th century BC by the Persian wars, during which Peparithos remained neutral. However, immediately after the end of these wars it became a member of the First Athenian Confederacy or Delian League, and its contribution to the common treasury on Delos amounted to the sum of 3,000 talents. Following the example of the Athenians, it implemented a democratic system of government on the island, which played a special role in the history of Greece. The Peloponnesian War and the defeat of Athens, of which it was a loyal ally, placed it in a difficult position, because the Spartan victors imposed an oligarchic polity on it. It was subsequently conquered by Alexander, the tyrant of Pherres, and then by the Macedonians and the Romans, who permitted the restoration of democratic government. Trade began to flourish again, with wine exports bringing in considerable revenues.

The 2nd century AD brought the first reference to the island by the name of Skopelos (changing from the hitherto customary Peparithos) by astronomer Claudius Ptolemaeus, or Ptolemy, the greatest geographer of antiquity. Christianity spread to the island in the third century AD and in the middle of the 4th century an archbishop's see was established which would last until 1842. The first to occupy the post of archbishop was Reginos, who was later proclaimed a saint and protector of the island.

The fourth century also witnessed the beginning of the 800-year period of Byzantine rule. Very little historical evidence remains from this period, despite its long duration. It is nevertheless known that ancient Peparithos was abandoned during this time, as were the sites of other ancient towns on the island, and that new settlements, much smaller than the towns, came into existence at a number of different locations.

After the fall of Constantinople to the Latins in 1204, the Venetians occupied Skopelos and made it the seat of a barony. A long succession of lords became masters of the island, among whom was Philippo Ghisi, who simultaneously enjoyed leading the life of a pirate. In 1538 the Turkish pirate Khayr ad-Din (Barbarossa) put an end to Turkish sovereignty when he attacked the island with 150 ships, sacked it and killed the inhabitants. Skopelos lay devastated for many years until it was recolonised by new settlers, whom the Turks allowed to be self-governing, granting them certain other rights as well.

At the beginning of the 18th century a man of letters named Stefanos Daponte founded a school on the island. He and his family also assisted in the establishment of the famous monastery of Evangelistria (the Virgin of the Annunciation), which will be dealt with in greater detail in the section on monasteries. During the same century, in the course of the Russo-Turkish War, sailors from Skopelos fought alongside the Russians against the Turks in the crucial naval battle of Cesme (1770). In this battle the whole Turkish fleet went up in flames, with the result that the Russians became the dominant power in the Aegean until the signing of the peace treaty of Kutchuk Kainardji (1774) which restored the power of Turkey. But in the meantime the spirit of the Revolution was spreading throughout all of Greece and it was not long before the armed struggle began. Skopelos frequently provided refuge for the revolutionary fighters, it participated in the Revolution, and became part of liberated Greece in 1830 by virtue of the Protocol of London.

Culture and tradition

It isn't only the natural beauty of the island that attracts visitors to Skopelos; it is also the remarkable cultural heritage and its inhabitants' determination to preserve their traditions. You will see this at celebrations and on religious feast days when the women wear their handsome **traditional costume**: a long sleeveless silk dress with multicoloured embroidery around the edges; under it, a fine, short-sleeved silk chemise embroidered with gold, and a head-dress with hanging gold coins all round.

It is enjoyable to see the women dancing all together, not the balos, which is danced on the other islands, but chiefly the tsamikos or the kalamatianos, which have their roots on the central Greek mainland opposite, and in the Peloponnese.

Of particular interest are the island's **local celebrations.** The feasts and events that take place in the Hora are famed for their gaiety. The most famous of these is the feast of Ayios Reginos on 25 February, at the church of Skopelos's patron saint. Many people arrive the day before and remain there all night. On the feast day proper, after the service, homemade sweets and Turkish delight are offered. On 24 June, the feast of St John the Baptist is celebrated at the monastery of Ayios Ioannis Prodromos, 6 km from Hora. On the eve, there is a vigil and on the day itself, after the service, food is served. The same happens on 6 August at the monastery of the Metamorphosis (Transfiguration).

On 4 December the feast of St Barbara is celebrated at the monastery of Ayia Varvara, also 6 km from Hora. Here too a vigil is held on the previous evening. One difference is that the custom at this monastery is for baked fish to be served on the feast day after the service.

Other events are usually organised in August by the municipality. This cycle of events usually closes with the Plum Festival, which is also characterised by celebrating and dancing. The food served at this feast is baked plums and wine, which also happen to be the island's choicest products.

1

2

3

Skopelos is rich in folklore, elements of which you will see everywhere you go.
A good place to start is the Folklore Museum (see p. 87).

Don't miss a visit to some of the fine churches, approximately 380 in number, to be found on the island, or to one of the famous monasteries, set amid pine forests and gazing down at the sea from on high. Some of them are Byzantine monasteries, with wall paintings, superb carved wood icon screens and centuries-old icons. You can also visit the interesting archaeological sites at the temple of Asclepius, the tomb of Staphylos, Sentoukia, Panormos and Loutraki.

1. 1. Dances at Skopelos feasts.
2, 3. The chapel of the Virgin on Psathoura.
4. Interesting exhibits at the island's
   Folklore Museum.

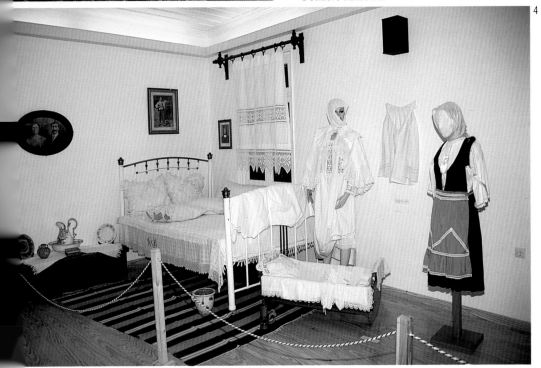

4

Skopelos Town (Hora)

From the very first moment you catch sight of the town of Skopelos (called Hora, or chief town, by the local people), you feel its enchantment. The town with its white houses climbing up to the top of the hill, with its countless churches, all set against the lush green background of the mountain: this is the picture that will remain imprinted on your memory. You will want to get out into the port as soon as possible and wander through its narrow streets. Besides being the main point of reference, the port of Skopelos is also the focal point of most of the activities on the island. Starting from the port, you can climb to the top of the hill on which ancient Peparithos was built in the second millennium BC. But to get there, you have to cross the town, walking through its picturesque little streets, with its two-storey and three-storey houses, some of which are very old and show the Venetian influence in their architecture. This influence is also evident from the name of the district in which they are situated: Frangomahalas, i.e. the quarter (mahalas) of the Franks (or Europeans). The newer houses have been more strongly influenced by the architecture of Thessaly or even Macedonia. Frequently you'll see the floor above the ground floor projecting out into the street, with the overhanging part supported on wooden posts. But all these

houses blend together here harmoniously. What they have in common is their balconies, their verandahs and their courtyards filled with flowers.

You continue on through the streets, climbing up some steps until you reach the top. This site is called Kastro today, taking its name from the fortress built here in 340 BC by Philip II of Macedonia, the father of Alexander the Great, on the ruins of ancient Peparithos. The fortress underwent various modifications until it was repaired for the last time by the Ghisi family in the 13th century. Nothing but the ruins of its walls have survived to the present day. Inside the Kastro is the oldest church in Hora, Ayios Athanasios. It is an aisleless basilica with 17th-century wall paintings. The initial edifice was constructed in the 9th century, on the ruins of a temple of Athena. Before leaving the Kastro let us take one last look at the panoramic view which opens out before us. Many years ago all the roofs of the houses were made of grey slate tiles which slanted down on four sides from the top. Rows of semi-cylindrical terracotta tiles used to be placed, open side down, along the ridges thus created and painted white. The contrast made the whole town look like something out of a fairy-tale. Today the grey slate has been replaced by red terracotta tiles and the stark whitewashed ridges (called kavalarides or "riders") have become a rare sight. Yet, despite this change, the Hora of Skopelos with its 3,000 inhabitants remains one of the most picturesque towns in the Aegean and has justly been designated a heritage settlement.

The town of Hora on Skopelos looks like a fairy tale even in an age when nobody believes in fairy tales.

The churches and monasteries of Hora

On the way down from the Kastro, you should pay a visit to some of island's most notable churches. There are said to be 123 churches in the town, 20 of which are in the Kastro, with an estimated total of 380 churches on the island. Among the most noteworthy of these churches are those of Zoodohos Pigi, Ayios Michalis Synadon, the aisleless basilicas of Ayios Athanasios, Ayios Nikolaos and the Ayioi Apostoloi, as well as the churches of Ayios Georgios, Ayios Dimitrios, Christos and the Panayitsa, which is built on a rock at the edge of the port. West of the town is the Monastery of the Episkopi (Bishopric) and to the south is the church and tomb of Ayios Reginos, the island's patron saint and first bishop who was martyred in 362 AD.

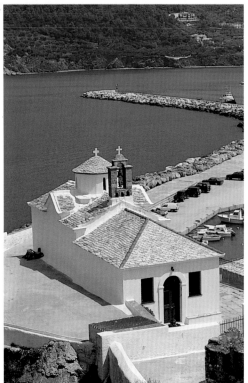

The island's main monasteries are mainly situated to the east of Hora. The closest monastery to Hora, with the exception of course of the Episkopi, is the 17th century Panayia Livadiotissa. One of the most important monasteries on the island is the Evangelistria which was built in 1712 on the ruins of an older monastery. But the convent of Ayios Ioannis Prodromos (John the Baptist), and the monasteries of Ayia Varvara (Saint Barbara) and the Metamorphosis (Transfiguration) are also significant even though they are only open on their feast days, and closed for the rest of the year.

1. The monastery of the Transfiguration.
2. The monastery of St John the Baptist.
3. The church of Panayia in Hora,
   the so-called Panayitsa.

Other sites in Hora

To the east of the harbour, half submerged in the sea at the location known as Ambeliki, is the Asclepeio. These ruins are all that has been preserved of the 4th century BC temple of Asclepius and its ancillary buildings. Other places worth a visit in Hora are the pottery workshop of Rhodios, the house of the writer Pavlos Nirvanas and above all the **Folklore Museum**. The Folklore Museum is housed in a traditional three-storey building furnished and decorated by local craftsmen in the traditional idiom. Their aim was to create a faithful representation of the traditional Skopelitan household. In the basement of the building there is a collection of agricultural implements used by the local farmers. The sitting room is on the ground floor, complete with hearth and decorated with attractive plates produced in Skopelos. On the first floor is the living room and beside it the bedroom, adorned with a display of the island's celebrated embroidery. The second floor houses the studio of the late Yiannis Lemonis, the traditional craftsman. He used to make tiny ornamental knives, but unfortunately had no one to follow him in this singular craft. Thus the few exquisite examples of his artistry that you can see in the museum are the last of their kind.

The nearest beach for swimming is at **Glyfoneri or Ayios Konstantinos** to the north of the town. Farther north is **Glysteri Bay**. Both of these places are accessible by car or by caique from the port. From Glysteri you can visit the nearby Tripiti cave. It is possible to go by boat into one of the entrances to the cave and come out the other. But most visitors prefer the sandy beach of Staphylos, which is sheltered from the meltemi wind and is no more than four kilometres away. Some go to other beaches which are farther off and about which we shall have more to say later. Regarding transportation, here is a regular bus service to and from Staphylos and the other beaches on the island's southern coast.

1, 2. Views of the Folkore Museum.
3, 4. The village and beach of Glysteri.

Tour of the island

On Skopelos you can visit beautiful beaches such as those at Staphylos, Valanio, Agnondas, Milia, and Elios, idyllic locations like Panormos, and the picturesque villages of Klima, Atheato, and Glossa with its port of Loutraki. Opposite Panormos is forest-green Dassia which offers yet another option.

Staphylos - Valanio - Agnondas

Staphylos is the favourite beach of everyone who lives in Hora, given that it is only four kilometres from the town. It a beautiful beach with a calm sea, sheltered from the meltemi winds. At the same time, it is perhaps the island's most important archaeological and historical site. All around it, a dense pine forest extends almost to the sea. In between are greyish-red rocks and then stretching out round the cove is a great horseshoe-shaped sandy beach washed by the clear blue waters. At the southern end of the beach there is a small headland, rocky but also quite verdant, which is linked to the rest of the mainland by a narrow neck of land about ten metres high. On one side it is forested, on the other it is bare and precipitous, with colours shading from pink through brown and red.

The leeward beach of Staphylos.

This neck of land is full of surprises. Behind it is a second beach, **Valanio** beach, perhaps even more beautiful than the first. The name derives from balineum, the ancient Latin word for bath. You are now at the highest point of the path that links these two bays. However many books one may have read on the history of these parts, it is one thing to read about a place and another to see it with one's own eyes. Somewhere near this very path, traces were found of an ancient edifice which may well have been the palace of the legendary Staphylos, the emissary of Minos who become the first settler on the island and its first king. To the left and right are the two beaches

and in front, the small headland.

It was here at the base of the headland that the famous royal tomb was found containing a veritable archaeological treasure trove: weapons, gold jewellery, vases, a double-headed axe, and above all a sword hilt embellished with gold. This was a king's sword which has been attributed to Staphylos, because all the finds, which date from the 16th century BC, appear to be Minoan. Here myth blends with history and becomes one with it. It seems reasonable that the Minoan prince and his brother Peparithos, on their voyage from Crete, would have disembarked at the bay of Staphylos, the southernmost bay on the island and well sheltered from the north winds, rather than seeking anchorage elsewhere. This train of thought is reinforced by another point worth mentioning. On the headland, traces of an ancient settlement have been found. Was it there that ancient Peparithos was initially built, only to be evacuated subsequently and re-established on the present-day site of Hora?

We leave picturesque Staphylos, following the paved road that covers the entire length of the island. The road turns temporarily away from the sea to descend four kilometres later to beautiful **Agnondas** beach. This is another name from antiquity; it was given to the bay by its ancient inhabitants in honour of their compatriot Agnonas, who in 569 BC won a race in the Olympic Games. Agnondas, eight kilometres from Hora, is the island's third largest port after Skopelos and Loutraki, the harbour of Glossa. It is here that ships anchor when weather conditions prevent them from approaching the harbour of Skopelos. It is a village with a beautiful sandy beach, hotels, tavernas and rooms to rent.

A magnificent bay, **Limnonari**, is situated only a short distance away to the northwest. You can get there by caique or on foot, following the path overlooking the sea. The hillside above the bay is rocky. Hidden in the cove is a fine beach. There is such a profusion of pine trees surrounding it on all sides that their reflection in the water makes the sea look green.

Panormos - Milia - Elios

From Agnondas the road turns away from the sea again bringing you to the idyllic **Panormos** region, nine kilometres later. Before coming out on the main bay we pass alongside a narrow cove, a delightful little fjord which bears no resemblance to the fjords of Norway as it is lavishly covered with pine trees, and the sunlight on the sea colours it the most amazing blue. As you descend to the beachfront at Panormos, you will see a colorful picture. The bay is enclosed with two small islands at its entrance. The larger one, resembling a green cone, is called Dassia. Behind the beach of pebbles and coarse sand there are a few hotels and tavernas. Next to the sea, but in a fairly inaccessible location, there are traces of ancient walls. Panormos is seventeen kilometres from Hora.

From Panormos the road begins an uphill climb, following the coastline as before. Between it and the sea is a slope with a sparse cover of pine trees descending gently to the coast and continuing to the west as far as the headland at the entrance to Panormos bay. At that point everything changes. The coastline swings northwards and becomes precipitous, almost perpendicular. The pine forest becomes denser, with trees suspended over the sea, now of the brightest azure. This is the beginning of the celebrated Milia beach, one of the most beautiful in the Aegean. The view is best enjoyed from the road, which is now at its highest point. In any case you have to follow the road in order to get down to **Milia**. Here, looking down on it from above, the beach is a long ribbon of white, obscured here and there by the encroaching pine forest.

1, 2. The harbour and beach of Agnondas.
3. Limnonari.
4. Pine-covered Panormos.

4

Opposite is **Dassia**, the greenest of green islets, to complete the marvellous landscape.

The beach extends for a kilometre and is accessible by means of a side road which branches off when the main road has come down to the level of the coast. It is worth mentioning here that during the height of the tourist season in the summer months, this beach, the finest on the island, is covered with multi-coloured umbrellas and deck-chairs and of course, people.

The road continues towards the northern part of the island, running parallel to the coast. Vegetation is lush on the hillsides, making for a most enjoyable journey. Approximately three kilometres past Milia we -

1

2

-come to **Elios**, which has a sandy beach and a recently built village by the name of **Neo Klima**. It was established by the inhabitants of the village of Kato Klima which was destroyed by landslides. Its houses are all new, with roofs of concrete but sometimes also of terracotta tiles. In a clearing facing the sea a little wharf has been built for boats, with a small breakwater to protect it. There are a handful of hotels in Nea Klima, and many houses with rooms for rent.

1. The beach at Milia.
2. The village of Neo Klima.
3, 4. Panormos and Dassia.
5. The beach of Elios.

Klima - Glossa - Loutraki

After Elios and Neo Klima the road continues in a northwesterly direction, always on a hill overlooking the sea, as it passes through **Klima** and Pano Klima. The houses here have been built amphitheatrically on the slopes of the mountain. After Pano Klima the road turns away from the coast towards the interior of the island.

We go past the village of Atheato and through the hamlet of Mahalas, to arrive finally in Glossa, the second largest village on Skopelos with approximately 1,300 inhabitants. **Glossa** is built on the side of a mountain 250 metres above the sea. It is surrounded on all sides by pine forests, fruit trees such as plum and almond trees, with plane trees in the ravines. There are so many plane trees that the old name for the village was Platana, from the Greek word for this tree. It is said that the word Glossa may be derived from Knossa, a name reminiscent of Knossos, and may have been bestowed on it by the island's Minoan colonists. It's worth taking a stroll through the streets of the village, with its two-storey houses surveying the sea from their lofty look-out point. Their architectural style recalls that of Macedonia with its wooden balconies and terracotta-tile roofs. And if it happens to be a feast day, you will see women in the streets in their handsome traditional finery. This costume is also worn at the dance on the feast of the Assumption of the Virgin (15th August) or at the "Loïzeia", the commemorative celebrations held at the beginning of August each year to commemorate the late composer Manos

Loïzos, who spent many of his summers in Glossa. A kilometre from the village is the Byzantine monastery of the Taxiarches (Archangels), a dependent monastery (metochion) of Mount Athos. The monastery's katholikon contains a remarkable carved wood icon screen. On the windswept northern coasts of the island, to the east of Glossa, stands the little chapel of Aï Yiannis or St John, constructed on the summit of a rock. This huge rock is like a small peninsula, linked to the mainland by a narrow neck of land. To get to the church one has to climb the 104 steps that have been hewn out of the rock.

The port of Glossa is named **Loutraki**, and is right below it, about two kilometres away. The road connecting the village with the port is full of hairpin curves and surrounded by a dense pine forest standing in reddish soil. Loutraki is the island's second port. Beyond the port, by the seaside, there are springs that supply the village with water. Ruins of Roman baths can be found at this location. But most significant, from an archaeological viewpoint, are the ruined walls of the citadel of ancient Selinous, dating from the 4th century BC, along with a temple of Athena from the 5th century. These are all to be found on a hilltop 300 metres northwest of the harbour. Loutraki offers both hotel accommodation and rooms to rent.

Here our tour of Skopelos comes to an end. We may now return to Hora and from there arrange our departure, or else take the boat from Loutraki and bid farewell to this lovely island.

1. The little harbour of Paleo Klima.
2. Verdant Loutraki.
3, 4. Glossa.
5. The little church of Aï Yianni at Glossa.

The sea-bed around Alonnisos is among the most beautiful to be found in the Aegean Sea. Imagine white marble, streaked with red, descending into emerald waters in column-like formations, and over the rock a dense forest of pine. This is the picture you will encounter on most of the island's coasts, but you will find it at its most beautiful at Votsi, the bay just to the north of the harbour of Patitiri. The old capital – Horio (village) or Liadromia, as it is called by the locals – was built high up on the hilltop and remains apart from the hustle and bustle of the tourist traffic. There, despite the damage wrought by the 1965 earthquake, some of the old traditional houses have been preserved, some have been renovated by their new owners, and others abandoned to the ravages of time. Most of the inhabitants of the village evacuated their houses after the earthquake, sold them to foreigners and built a new settlement farther down the hillside, near the sea.It seems that Alonnisos was once part of another island called Kyra-Panayia, or even more

ealing nature

likely, part of the island of Psathoura, where there are ruins of an ancient city on the sea floor nearby. Both of these islands are to the north of Alonnisos and were once all joined together in a single island. Alonnisos has been inhabited since pre-historic times. One important settlement was the ancient city of Ikos (at the site of present-day Kokkino-kastro), where sections of the acropolis walls have been preserved from the period of classical antiquity. In the 4th century BC there were numerous conflicts between the Athenians and Philip of Macedonia over possession of Alonnisos. The island was more important than Skiathos but less so than neighbouring Skopelos. It was in fact dependent on the latter and shared its fortunes. In the 2nd century AD it was occupied by the Romans. The period of Byzantine rule followed during which the castle walls of Horio were built, and in 1207 the island was captured by the Venetian family of Ghisi. The Turks gained possession of the island in 1538; it became part of the newly constituted modern Hellenic state in 1830.

Geography

Alonnisos is not far from Skopelos and just 62 nautical miles from Volos. With a dense cover of pine forest – the trees frequently suspended over the sea – the island is 64 square kilometres in area, with 64 kilometres of coastline and a population of 1,500. None of its mountains are over 500 metres high. The vineyards of Alonnisos are famous for their choice wine, and herbs used for medicinal purposes thrive in its soil.

There are a large number of small islands near Alonnisos. These islands, with their sea caves, offer a refuge to Mediterranean monk seals (Monachus monachus).

In the region there is a park entitled Alonisos-Northern Sporades National Maritime Park, which is regarded as a highly significant breeding ground for this rare species of seal, which is among the six mammal species on the planet that are considered endangered. The seals and their pups find refuge in the coastal caves that have been created by the action of the waves on the region's limestone rock.

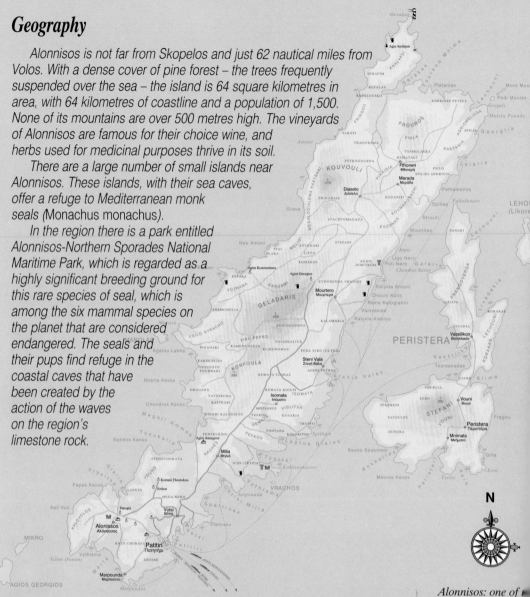

Alonnisos: one of few earthly paradis

Getting to know the island

On Alonnisos one can visit **Palio Horio** or **Liadromia** which is about 4 kms from the port, on the top of a steep hill with a fantastic view. The earthquake in 1965 destroyed most of the houses. On the edge of the cliff some parts of the old Byzantine wall have been preserved, which was later repaired by the Ghisi family of Venetian conquerors.

Of considerable interest are the churches which survived the earthquake, such as the Byzantine chapel of Ayioi Anargyroi, which you'll find after a delightful walk. At Ayios Andreas of Alonnisos is the headquarters of the International Academy of Homeopathic Medicine where people can find information about alternate forms of treatment that promise solutions to many health problems.

Views of Alonnisos.

*A walk around **Patitiri** is a must; it is the island's port and the harbour of Hora. Its houses are built on the rocks in an amphitheatrical formation, with dense pine forest all around.*

*   **Votsi**, which is situated one kilometre northeast of Patitiri, is a settlement that overlooks the most picturesque bay on the island, including the little harbour with its romantic tavernas.*

Views of Patitiri and Votsi.

Aerial photograph of Patitiri and Votsi.

Chrysi Milia: One of the most beautiful beaches on Alonnisos, four kilometres northeast of Patitiri. The trip there by caique (from Patitiri) takes about twenty minutes.

Kokkinokastro: A sandy beach situated beneath an abruptly rising neck of land northeast of Patitiri, with reddish soil and pine trees on its crest. Not far away one can see the crumbling walls of an ancient city which is believed to have been the celebrated Ikos. Daily excursions come here in summer.

Kokkinonisi or Vrahos: An islet opposite Kokkinokastro. Tools from the Palaeolithic era were found here and are considered to be the earliest evidence of human habitation in the Aegean.

Tzortzi Yialos: A fine beach, immediately after Kokkinokastro. Some believe that the port of the ancient town of Ikos was situated here.

Leptos Yialos: A picturesque small bay with pure white sand and very clean water, six km. northeast of Patitiri, or thirty minutes by caique.

Steni Vala: A settlement fronting a narrow inlet, resembling a small fjord. It is developing into a tourist resort. Located twelve kilometres northeast of Patitiri.

Marpounda: A tourist resort with two excellent beaches as well as a rocky seafront, at the southern-most point of Alonnisos, three km from Patitiri.

Beautiful beaches on Alonnisos. Lakkes (1), Kokkinokastro (2), Chrysi Milia (3) Megalos Myrtias (4), Steni Vala (5), Marpounda (6).

Islets near Alonnisos

Yioura: A mountainous, inaccessible island, well known for the celebrated cave of the Cyclops, with its stalagmites and stalactites, in the western part of the island. To get to the cave, the service of a guide is required. A rare species of wild goat similar to the Cretan kri kri lives on this island. Yioura is northeast of Alonnisos, between Kyra-Panayia and Psathoura.

Dio Adelfia (Two Brothers): Two small islands that are visible to the east of Patitiri. They are between Alonnisos and Skantzoura.

Kyra-Panayia (Pelagonisi): The largest and most interesting of the islets around Alonnisos. Some say that it was the ancient Alonnisos. It has three bays: Ayios Petros in the southwest with its fine sandy beaches; Planitis in the north, a superb natural closed harbour; and a smaller harbour in the east, where the monastery of the Virgin Mary (Panayia) is located, a building which probably dates from the 16th century. Its katholikon is an aisleless basilica; it also has monks' cells, a refectory and a guest house. The monastery is a dependency of the Megistis Lavras monastery on Mount Athos. The few inhabitants of Kyra-Panayia raise animals here. The island is 12 nautical miles northeast of Alonnisos and is accessible by means of the caiques which come on excursions from Patitiri.

Peristera (Xero): The closest to Alonnisos and the second largest islet after Kyra-Panayia, it has lovely sandy coves, very few inhabitants and two natural harbours, Vasiliko and Peristeri.

Piperi: A verdant little island in the middle of the Aegean, the most distant of these small islets from Alonissos and lashed by all the winds. The caique which goes from Patitiri to Kyra-Panayia only infrequently continues as far as Piperi. A rare breed of small-bodied cow, cinnamon and black in colour and of the so-called shorthorn breed, can be found on the island.

Pappous: *A small islet with an attractive old church on it. It is situated between Kyra-Panayia and Yioura, alongside the islet of Prasso.*

Skantzoura: *The island is well-known to fishermen, especially spear-fishermen. It is 13 nautical miles southeast of Alonissos, has good beaches and a monastery with guest accommodation. Its only inhabitants are shepherds.*

Psathoura: *The northernmost of the Alonissos islets, and indeed, of all the Sporades. It is so low in elevation that it is difficult to see from a distance. At night, however, its lighthouse, built on the volcanic rock, makes its presence known to passing ships. Off the southern part of the island, near the port and between Psathoura and the small islet of Psathouropoula, is an ancient city, submerged beneath the sea and identified by some as ancient Alonissos.*

1. *Kyra Panayia on Erimonisi.*
2, 3, 4. *Psathoura.*

USEFUL INFORMATION

How to get to Skiathos

Skiathos can be reached by sea or air. Visitors to Greece, wherever they are in the country, can make their way by road to the harbours of the Greek mainland, Thessaly or Evia that are near Skiathos, and then cross over to the island by ferry.

By plane

Olympic Airways has many daily flights from Athens to the island in summer, with somewhat fewer in winter. The flight lasts forty minutes. The airport of Skiathos is situated two to four kilometres northeast of Hora near the Vromovrisi district. Passengers are transported to and from Hora by either O.A. bus or by the public (KTEL) buses. A taxi service is likewise available. There are charter flights to Skiathos from other countries.

Information: Olympic Airways, tel. (301) 9616161 (Athens), tel. (0427) 22270 and (0427) 22229 (Skiathos), Skiathos Airport, tel. (0427) 22049.

By ship

Every day in summer there are one or more scheduled ferryboat departures for Skiathos, with somewhat fewer in winter, from Ayios Konstantinos (near Kammena Vourla). The distance is 44 miles (three and a half hours). There is a daily service from Volos to Skiathos, a distance of 42 miles (three and a half hours). In summer Skiathos has connections with Alonnisos and Skopelos, Skyros, Thessaloniki, Tinos, Mykonos, Paros, Ios, Santorini and Herakleio, Crete. There is also a daily service from Thessaloniki to Skiathos. A boat departs from Kymi in Evia, a distance of 49 miles or six hours, three times a week.

Information: Athens office, tel. 3622093, 3632575; Ayios Konstantinos office, tel. (0235) 31920 and 31989. Skiathos office,

(0427) 22204. Volos port authority, tel. (041) 28888. Kymi office in Athens, tel. 3623228, 3622093, 3632575. Kymi port authority, tel. (0222) 22606.

By Flying Dolphin

Flying dolphins (hydrofoils) depart for Skiathos every day from Ayios Konstantinos, Volos, Thesssaloniki, Halkidiki, Evia, Pelion, Skopelos and Alonnisos. From Ayios Konstantinos the trip takes an hour and a half. From Volos it takes an hour and twenty minutes.

Information: Central agency in Piraeus, tel. 4527107, in Ayios Konstantinos (0235) 31614 and 31874, in Volos tel. (0421) 39786 and 39787 and in Skiathos (0427) 22018.

By road

There is a KTEL bus service from Athens to Ayios Konstantinos (a distance of 166 kilometres).

Information: KTEL, tel. 8317147 and 8317158.

From Athens to Kymi, KTEL buses cover the distance of 167 km. in 4 hours.

Information: KTEL: tel. 8317163.

Both KTEL buses and OSE railways go from Athens to Volos.

Information: KTEL: 8317186 and OSE (Greek railways) tel. 9231514.

On Skiathos

There is good public transport on the island. A bus service connects Hora with Koukounaries, Kanapitsa and Troulos, with stops at various points on the coast and at other intermediate destinations. The same route can be made by taxi. There are also caiques making the trip round the island's coastal settlements (Achladies, Kanapitsa, Megali Ammos, Kalamaki, Troulos,